posters

The Collection of the International Red Cross
and Red Crescent Museum

musée + (genève
www.redcrossmuseum.ch

SilvanaEditoriale

Contents

"Tell them"[1]

Roger Mayou

Shortly after the International Red Cross and Red Crescent Museum opened, it received on loan the entire collection of posters owned by the International Federation of Red Cross and Red Crescent Societies. That collection has been added to over time with purchases and gifts. With over 10,000 pieces, the Museum is now the recognized authority on these objects. The posters rotate regularly through a dedicated space in the permanent exhibition.

The oldest poster in the collection dates back to 1866, three years after the Red Cross was founded. It calls for donations for soldiers, as would the majority of posters produced up to the First World War.

But following the unspeakable carnage of that conflict, in which some ten million soldiers – and possibly just as many civilians – perished, the global community sought to prevent future wars of that scale. New institutions intended to keep the peace, such as the League of Nations, were created.

> True mirrors of society, these posters reflect the concerns of the era that produced them

For their part, the National Red Cross and Red Crescent Societies deliberated how they could be useful in times of peace. They had acquired considerable expertise and a multitude of well-trained volunteers, and the disaster of the First World War was far from over: famine, typhus and influenza were spreading fast at a time of unprecedented mass displacement. So the National Societies decided to coordinate their activities – their aim was to respond to immediate health crises and natural disasters, of course, but also to prevent future ones by promoting public health, hygiene, nutrition and first aid. They were driven by a desire to help mankind.

It was in this spirit that the League of Red Cross Societies was founded in 1919.[2] The League immediately recognized that it could use its extensive network to communicate around the globe. Drawing inspiration from the advertising world, it would disseminate its messages as widely as possible via one of the most modern media of the time: posters.

The Museum's collection is noteworthy in several regards. True mirrors of society, these posters reflect the concerns of the era that produced them, such as the fight against tuberculosis, malaria and AIDS, and, more recently, the vital importance of protecting our climate. And from a formal perspective, they show how communication strategies have evolved over time and the ways in which different cultures address similar topics.

The eight thematic chapters of this book present the National Societies' main activities as well as their appeals for both volunteers – particularly women and young people – and donations, a significant source of funding. The works were selected as much for their iconographic quality as for their historical value and regional interest.

In the age of social media, some commentators are quick to dismiss these images as visual pollution. Yet posters still cover the walls of our cities – proof of their enduring power.

[1] This title is taken from a poster produced by the Marshall Islands Red Cross Society in 2018 (see p. 171).

[2] Now the International Federation of Red Cross and Red Crescent Societies.

The Museum's poster collection: a reflection of humanitarian values

Field work is
about taking
action; museums
are about
conservation

Catherine Burer
Posters are things of the present – informing at a glance, seeking to persuade, and sometimes calling to action. The International Red Cross and Red Crescent Movement has used posters to introduce and promote itself to the public since 1866, the date of the earliest example in our collection. The ideal medium for communicating a message, a warning, or useful information, posters are inexpensive, can be printed anywhere and can reach a given group of people whenever needed, linking humanitarian organizations to their beneficiaries and donors. They are an important part of the Movement's heritage, a testament to both its past and its present.

The Museum's mission is to conserve the Movement's heritage: to protect and enrich it, to display it and to pass it along. The poster collection is a major highlight. Many of our posters come from National Red Cross and Red Crescent Societies, which work to promote health, prevent and fight epidemics, provide aid during natural disasters, and support communities through social action in peacetime. Two thirds of our National Society posters come from European countries and the rest from Asia, the Americas, Africa and Oceania. Nearly every country in the world has a National Society under the leadership of the International Federation of Red Cross and Red Crescent Societies. Their on-the-ground knowledge and experience – and their close ties to local communities – make them uniquely capable of providing aid where it's needed. The Museum holds posters from 159 of the 191 total National Societies in existence. Through partnerships with a number of them, we regularly receive examples of their products. Some of our posters come from the International Committee of the Red Cross, whose missions are to provide aid and assistance during armed conflicts and other situations of violence and to promote international humanitarian law and the Movement's fundamental principles. The remainder of our collection was acquired at auction or from private collectors and specialized galleries.

This book is organized thematically, and each section reflects a different aspect of the Movement's activities. The issues and concerns represented in the posters vary depending on the geographic, social and political context, but the message of humanity and peace is constant and universal. Recruitment, volunteerism, fundraising, blood drives and the promotion of junior chapters are also common threads.

Field work is about taking action; museums are about conservation. We document everything as precisely as possible. Many of the posters in our collection cannot be dated with any precision, however – they are first and foremost tools of the trade, products of the moment. Likewise, many of their designers are unknown. Although some were created by well-known figures such as Otto Baumberger, Jules Courvoisier, Ludwig Hohlwein, Viktor Koretsky, Lawrence Wilbur and Jes Schlaikjer, most are the work of little-known or anonymous artists.

The collection is in many ways a conceptually consistent whole, but it is made up of a diverse range of styles, formats, and cultures of origin. Posters from India, South Africa, Papua New Guinea and the Philippines, for example, tell entire stories in a highly descriptive style;

they take time to read. In the West, however, the posters tend to feature a large picture paired with a brief message in a striking font; their aim is to attract attention and be read quickly in a public space already saturated with information and images. Blood drive posters serve the same purpose in all countries, but their way of addressing donors and the atmosphere created by their graphic design can be radically different. The multitude of information, appeals and messages – intended for very different audiences – and the wide variety of aesthetic sensibilities represented all speak to the collection's formal, cultural and historical richness.

These images shock, stir up emotions and inspire action, perfectly fulfilling their original purpose: to raise awareness

The posters' aim is always to represent the work of the Red Cross and Red Crescent, though their focus changes visibly with the times. Part of what makes this collection so fascinating from an artistic, historical and sociological point of view is how the posters tell a story and reflect the ways the world has changed. From 1916 to the late 1960s, tuberculosis control is a dominant theme. Starting in the 1980s, however, the new menace of HIV/AIDS takes centre stage. When it comes to preventing illness, taboos are swept aside in every culture, and clear advice and instructions are given: "spitting is dangerous" or "don't kick up dust" in the case of tuberculosis. Later, in the age of HIV/AIDS, the walls are covered with giant images of condoms and with taglines such as "protect yourself, use a condom", "don't believe rumours, know the facts", and "information

– your first defence against AIDS". These clear messages urge everyone to take responsibility for their actions. The posters serve to convey information, but also to raise awareness and promote greater understanding. For many years, for instance, the goal in the wake of natural disasters such as hurricanes was on fundraising to bolster assistance efforts. More recently, however, posters have served to provide information and advice so that those affected can better protect themselves. Their stance is proactive, and their informative presence directly contributes to lowering the number of casualties. Rather than enjoining people to "give" or "help", they might instead read: "The mangroves: don't cut them down... your lives depend on them!"

Historical and social context determines which stories are told and which subjects are represented. Take, for example, the iconic image of the hard-working nurse, which was long an important metaphor for humanitarian work, representing the values of compassion and solidarity from the battlefields of the 19th century until as recently as the 1960s. She is the embodiment of service and symbolized the very essence of the Movement. Such imagery is no longer used today, though posters still speak of aid, commitment and the investment of people and resources. More recently, the tone has become less heroic and idealistic. Instead, posters seek to grab the viewer's attention through stark realism, as in the ICRC's "It's a matter of life and death" campaign (see p. 158). These images shock, stir up emotions and inspire action, perfectly fulfilling their original purpose: to raise awareness. And they do it well, communicating clearly in every style and language. It should be noted that the selection presented in this book does not illustrate the full range of the Museum's collection: no posters on the prevention of traffic accidents or household safety have been included, for example, despite being among the issues addressed by National Societies.

These posters show how humanitarian aid has changed over the course of history and signal the arrival of new challenges. Informational posters about the dangers of anti-personnel mines began to appear in the 1990s, for instance. The remarkable collage of portraits featured in "#NotATarget" from 2017 (see p. 167) reflects anxieties for the safety of Movement staff in a world where the most basic tenets of the Geneva Conventions – and the protective power they confer upon the Movement's symbols – are not always respected. Other ICRC posters evoke the right to dignity in detention or the issue of child soldiers: other signs that we live in a world that can sometimes lose its bearings.

Every one of these posters contributes to telling and illustrating a single story: the work and objectives of an organization focused on helping humanity. They are not trying to sell anything; their purpose is to inform, to educate and hopefully to encourage acts of altruism and solidarity. The activities and work they portray are in no way superfluous – they are at once practical and idealistic. These posters exist entirely outside of consumer culture, translating the desire to help, to alleviate human suffering, to improve quality of life

and to promote social consciousness, tolerance and peace. In short, to make the world more human. They reflect humanitarian values and the work of the Red Cross and Red Crescent, and are a testament to their constant evolution.

They are not trying to sell anything; their purpose is to inform, to educate and hopefully to encourage acts of altruism and solidarity

The activities and work they portray are in no way superfluous – they are at once practical and idealistic

1

"Serving humanity"

J.P. Gonzalez
Serving humanity...
Guatemala, n.d.
50 x 42 cm
MICR/BBT-1986-28-131

Alonso E. Foringer →
*The greatest mother
in the world*
USA, 1918
69 x 51.5 cm
MICR/BBT-1987-91-6

Agostinelli
*Peruvian Red Cross,
60th anniversary,
1879–17 April 1939*
Peru, 1939
81 x 57 cm
MICR/BBT-1986-28-205

The
GREATEST MOTHER
in the WORLD

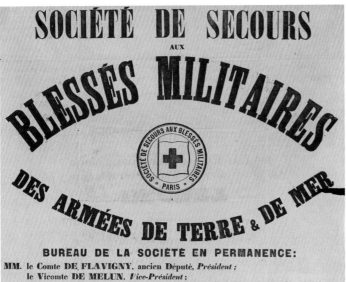

Unknown
For people's health – 35th anniversary
of the People's Health Protection Agency
Mongolia, 1960
41 x 59 cm
MICR/BBT-2001-16-73

Fernand Allard l'Olivier
Congolese Red Cross
Belgium, 1924
61 x 79 cm
MICR/BBT-2001-19-99

Unknown
*No borders for
the Red Cross*
Lebanon, n.d.
50 x 34 cm
MICR/BBT-1988-26-2

الصليب الأحمر
لا يعرف حدودًا

**PAS DE FRONTIERES
POUR LA CROIX ROUGE**

Unknown
*Vietnam Red Cross. 8 May,
World Red Cross Day*
Vietnam, n.d.
61 x 100 cm
MICR/BBT-2006-33-54

Unknown
Caring and sharing
Tonga, n.d.
98 x 65 cm
MICR/BBT-2002-29-100

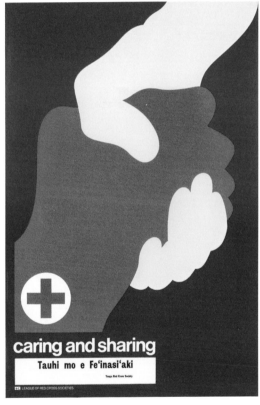

Unknown
*The Egyptian Red Crescent
Society is serving humanity in
peace and in war. Blood donations:
to save lives. Relief operations:
to ease humanitarian disasters.
Youth health services: a secure
refuge for humanity's future*
Egypt, n.d.
70 x 49 cm
MICR/BBT-1988-57-5

Croix-Rouge Monegasque

← Jean-Michel Folon
Red Cross of Monaco
Monaco, n.d.
80 x 60 cm
MICR/BBT-1995-93-1

Kouamé
Wanted for its principles
A unique face inspired by the seven Fundamental Principles:
Humanity, Impartiality, Neutrality, Independence, Voluntary Service,
Unity and Universality.
Togo, 1987
46 x 32 cm
MICR/BBT-1989-28-2

Hergé studio
More humanity, more peace
Belgium, 1984
30 x 20 cm
MICR/BBT-1988-84-3

Unknown
Humanity, Neutrality,
Impartiality, Independence,
Voluntary Service, Unity,
Universality, 80th anniversary
of the Estonia Red Cross,
1919–1999
Estonia, 1999
42 x 30 cm
MICR/BBT-2000-121-3

Unknown
Namibia Red Cross. Caring
for people and promoting
development
Namibia, n.d.
59.5 x 42 cm
MICR/BBT-1995-121-1

Unknown
South Sudan
Red Cross Society
South Sudan, 2017
164 x 60 cm
MICR/BBT-2017-33-1

South Sudan
Red Cross

Relief Distribution

Restoring Family Links

Social Mobilization

Psychosocial support to SSRC staff and volunteers

الهلال الأحمر التونسي

في خدمة الإنسانية

Unknown
*Tunisian Red Crescent,
serving humanity*
Tunisia, n.d.
44.5 x 32.5 cm
MICR/BBT-2001-40-56

Gokhan Eryoldhas, →
*A glimmer of hope.
Turkish Red Crescent
Society*
Turkey, 1964
82 x 56 cm
MICR/BBT-2001-65-71

Sanziz
*8 May 1977, Friendship Day,
Red Lion and Sun Society of
Iran Youth Organization*
Islamic Republic of Iran, 1977
57.2 x 41.5 cm
MICR/BBT-2006-28-33

١٨ اردیبهشت ٢٥٣٦
روز دوستی
سازمان جوانان شیر و خورشید سرخ ایران

ÜMİT IŞIĞI **KIZILAY**

GÖKHAN ERYOLDAŞ

KIRAL MATBAASI - ISTANBUL - Tel: 27 39 69

2

"You too can give!"

Ray Greenleaf
Answer the Red Cross Christmas roll call
USA, 1918
71 x 46.5 cm
MICR/BBT-2014-2

Answer the

Red Cross

Christmas Roll Call

All you need is a heart and a dollar

Ray Greenleaf

SEMANA DE LA CRUZ ROJA ARGENTINA
1880 - 10 de Junio - 1951
¡ASOCIESE!

Unknown
Argentine Red Cross Week.
Join! 1880 – 10 June 1951
Argentina, 1951
52 x 30 cm
MICR/BBT-2000-219-41

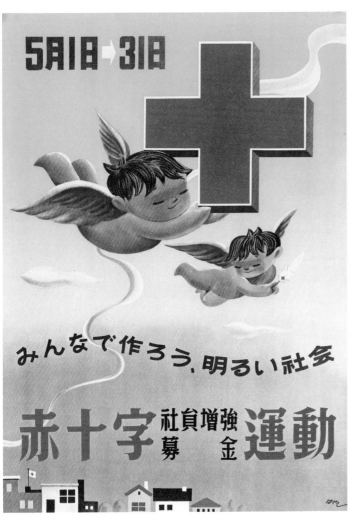

Unknown
1–31 May: Let's build a bright
society. Recruiting Red Cross
members and raising funds
Japan, n.d.
71.5 x 52 cm
MICR/BBT-2001-40-53

HELP THE RED CROSS

INDIAN RED CROSS SOCIETY

Printed By The ASIAN ART Printers Ltd Daryaganj New Delhi

Inde

← Anand
Help the Red Cross
India, n.d.
70.5 x 51 cm
MICR/BBT-1999-154-12

Jes Schlaikjer
*You too can help through
Red Cross*
USA, 1949
71 x 56 cm
MICR/BBT-1987-91-22

Puhlan Matbaasi
*Turkish philanthropy will spread
through the Red Crescent*
Turkey, 1956
70 x 50 cm
MICR/BBT-2000-218-58

Unknown
We protect your health! Help us!
Germany, 1963
59 x 42 cm
MICR/BBT-2000-219-1

Unknown
Help the Red Cross be ready: give!
Netherlands, 1953
53.5 x 38 cm
MICR/BBT-2000-219-52

Lars Bramberg
Swedish Red Cross, 1954 fundraiser
Sweden, 1954
99.5 x 69.5 cm
MICR/BBT-2001-7-78

M. Pisca
Red Cross Week
Croatia, 1951
100 x 70 cm
MICR/BBT-2003-42-15

N.C. Wyeth
Answer the call!
USA, 1953
48 x 38.5 cm
MICR/BBT-2007-12-1

Fritz Butz, Fred Troller
A light in the world
Switzerland, 1949
128 x 90 cm
MICR/BBT-1986-28-297

Geerts
All are brothers
Germany, n.d.
42 x 30 cm
MICR/BBT-2005-7-121

Unknown
5–31 May. Give to the Red Cross – together we must make the world better
Japan, n.d.
72.5 x 51 cm
MICR/BBT-2001-19-88

Unknown
Help us help others. Days of giving to the German Red Cross, 22 September to 5 October 1952
Germany, 1952
61 x 43 cm
MICR/BBT-2001-54-79

Unknown
...Hope for the future
Belgium, 1947
120.5 x 80 cm
MICR/BBT-2001-57-59

Unknown
The Red Cross is humanity's light – let us contribute
Republic of Korea, 1956
53.5 x 38.5 cm
MICR/BBT-2000-218-55

H. Beutler
*May 1952 fundraiser,
Swiss Red Cross*
Switzerland, 1952
23 x 18 cm
MICR/BBT-2005-29-10

Unknown
*The French Red Cross opens
the door to hope.
Join: 10 francs per year*
France, 1943
65 x 43 cm
MICR/BBT-2001-48-100

ВСТУПАЙТЕ
В ОБЩЕСТВА
КРАСНОГО
КРЕСТА И
КРАСНОГО
ПОЛУМЕСЯЦА!

Исполнительный комитет Союза обществ Красного Креста и Красного Полумесяца СССР
Л 101532 от 24/V-65 г.   Автор М. Б. МУКОМЕЛЬ.   Редактор Г. В. ГОЛЬДИНА   Художник Б. А. ГУСЕВ.
Цена 8 коп.   Издательское бюро треста Медучпособие   Типолит. ф-ка № 4 МУП Зак. 619. Тир. 100.000.

Souscription nationale
pour la
CROIX-ROUGE

Affiches "SONOR" S.A. Genève.

38

Unknown
*Colombian Red Cross week –
the needy await your aid*
Colombia, n.d.
70 x 50 cm
MICR/BBT-1999-154-11

Angel Esteban
*Spanish Red Cross –
Flag Day*
Spain, 1956
88 x 64.5 cm
MICR/BBT-2001-57-83

← Jules Courvoisier
*National fundraiser
for the Red Cross*
Switzerland, 1920
126 x 96 cm
MICR/BBT-1994-79-1

Ateliers Falbriard
*International Committee
of the Red Cross – For
victims of war – 1969
fundraiser*
Switzerland, 1969
127 x 90 cm
MICR/BBT-1986-28-309

Miles Harper
Think of the wounded!
United Kingdom, 1939–1945
30 x 20.5 cm
MICR/BBT-1987-11-1

Unknown
You too can give!
Switzerland, n.d.
17.5 x 21 cm
MICR/BBT-2005-10-28

Unknown
*Over 5 million people helped by
only 29,000 volunteers*
Mexico, 2006
40 x 60 cm
MICR/BBT-2011-43-1

Onemarketing.com
*"I'm a fan of the Red Cross.
Thanks to them, I feel safe at home."
Paul von Siebenthal, age 100,
independent retiree and fan of
the Red Cross Alarm*
Switzerland, 2016
170 x 119 cm
MICR/BBT-2017-8-4

Otto Baumberger
*Victims of war – the International
Committee of the Red Cross
is there to help them!*
Switzerland, 1943
128 x 90.5 cm
MICR/BBT-2018-23-3

K. Vegter
Relieve suffering: work for peace with The Netherlands Red Cross,
27 September–4 October fundraiser
Netherlands, 1924
109 x 80 cm
MICR/BBT-1986-28-194

Unknown
*The Turkish
Red Crescent Society
awaits your precious
contribution!*
Turkey, 1954
100 x 71 cm
MICR/BBT-2003-34-56

Kızılay,
Sizin kıymetli yardımınızı
bekliyor!

tombola nationale du niger
TRANCHE SPÉCIALE
DE LA
CROIX ROUGE

tirage le 4 décembre 1971

Eliha
Niger national lottery,
special Red Cross edition –
4 December 1971 drawing
Niger, 1971
60 x 45 cm
MICR/BBT-2006-33-62

Villalobos
Chilean Red Cross, Red Cross
Week – Aid campaign for abandoned
children – Let's help!
Chile, 1943
54.5 x 36.5 cm
MICR/BBT-2001-40-75

OFFREZ des cartes ☾

Fêtes
Mariages
Anniversaires

télégrammes illustrés

Zahia Bouchebaba
Gift cards: events, weddings,
birthdays – illustrated telegrams.
Algeria, n.d.
39 x 30.5 cm
MICR/BBT-2004-18-83

Fernand Allard l'Olivier
6 to 13 April 1924:
Belgian Red Cross Week
Belgium, 1924
105 x 64.5 cm
MICR/BBT-1986-28-62

Raimela
Red Cross Week
Finland, n.d.
100 x 71 cm
MICR/BBT-2003-27-95

Marinetti
Chilean Red Cross – in peace and in war – charity
Chile, 1930
67 x 51 cm
MICR/BBT-2001-65-78

Angel Esteban
Red Cross Lottery
Spain, 1957
69 x 49 cm
MICR/BBT-2000-218-63

Unknown
Call for support
Thailand, n.d.
54 x 39.5 cm
MICR/BBT-1987-34-74

Unknown
Red Crescent Week in Baghdad,
2–7 March 1940
Iraq, 1940
76 x 51.5 cm
MICR/BBT-2001-40-51

O. Kerhart
Become members of the Red Cross
Czech Republic, 1979
112 x 83 cm
MICR/BBT-2004-1-1

Harrison Fisher
Have you answered the Red Cross
Christmas roll call?
USA, 1918
76 x 70.5 cm
MICR/BBT-1987-91-15

Unknown
Help us to help others
Norway, n.d.
47 x 33 cm
MICR/BBT-2006-33-17

Unknown
Give
Canada, 1949
71 x 56 cm
MICR/BBT-2005-4-148

Unknown
You too can help the Red Cross serve – join
France, n.d.
58.5 x 38.5 cm
MICR/BBT-2001-5-64

Unknown
Give to the Red Cross,
18–24 September
Former Yugoslavia, 1938
64 x 48 cm
MICR/BBT-1987-34-92

Martin Jacoby-Boy
*Give! Days of sacrifice,
3–4–5 December 1915,
Berlin Red Cross*
Germany, 1915
140 x 95 cm
MICR/BBT-2003-59-1

← Jessie Wilcox Smith
*Have you a Red Cross
service flag?*
USA, 1918
71 x 53 cm
MICR/BBT-1987-91-11

J. Lonay
*Association of French ladies –
French Red Cross – Help us
care for our wounded, buy
stamps with images of our
generals*
France, 1914–1918
120 x 80 cm
MICR/BBT-1987-85-2

Unknown
A bit of home
United Kingdom, 1939–1945
36.50 x 25 cm
MICR/BBT-2003-10-22

ROTE KREUZ-SAMMLUNG
1914
SAMMLUNG ZUGUNSTEN DER FREI-
WILLIGEN KRANKENPFLEGE IM KRIEGE

BELGIAN ✚ RED CROSS

DONATIONS MAY BE SENT TO THE HON. TREASURER,
THE RHT. HON. THE LORD MAYOR OF LONDON,
OR TO THE PRESIDENT, BARON C. GOFFINET.
3, SAVOY COURT, LONDON, W. C.

COPIES OF THIS POSTER MAY BE OBTAINED PRICE 1/- EACH FROM 3, SAVOY COURT. W. C.

PRINTED BY JOHNSON, RIDDLE & CO., LTD., LONDON, S.E.

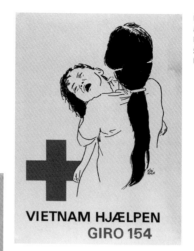

Kai Rich
Help Vietnam
Denmark, 1968
53.5 x 39 cm
MICR/BBT-2007-18-11

Unknown
The Red Cross is always with you! Japanese Red Cross Society, 1960 – Red Cross Movement
Japan, 1960
72 x 51 cm
MICR/BBT-1986-28-159

Norman Buena
The mangroves: don't cut them down... your lives depend on them!
Philippines, 1998
60 x 43.5 cm
MICR/BBT-2001-138-2

HIER
FEHLT
EINE
SCHULKISTE

Nahler
Missing: one school kit
Germany, 1965
33 x 24 cm
MICR/BBT-2000-218-33

Vor verden - Vort ansvar

Unknown
*Our world –
our responsibility*
Denmark, n.d.
50.5 x 35 cm
MICR/BBT-2002-13-44

Unknown
*Help Holland –
Account 154.*
Denmark, 1953
85 x 62.5 cm
MICR/BBT-2003-22-38

Unknown
Who will help the Red Cross?
National fundraiser,
7–20 March 2005
Mexico, 2005
40 x 60 cm
MICR/BBT-2011-43-6

Unknown
Help the victims
of disasters
Austria, n.d.
59 x 41 cm
MICR/BBT-2003-33-79

Unknown
Earthquake, tidal wave,
beware cyclone, flood, fire
Samoa, n.d.
61 x 40.5 cm
MICR/BBT-2003-30-16

The visual politics of Red Cross and Red Crescent posters

Valérie Gorin

Since the late 1800s, the posters produced by the International Committee of the Red Cross (ICRC) and the National Red Cross and Red Crescent Societies have been central to the imagery that marked the birth of humanitarian communications. What interests us here is the manner in which they illuminate their subject matter, that is, the visual elements and modes of representation employed across the decades. The visual politics of such images encompass the power relations constructed between the institution, the people represented and the public within a given era. The ICRC was founded in 1863 on the idea of humanizing war. The poster provided a means of elaborating on the principles at the core of the Red Cross's identity: foremost humanity, which is central to humanitarian action, as well as the operational principles of neutrality, impartiality and independence. Paintings and drawings reproduced in large format could show national audiences the new reality of aid work, in an imaginary realm drawing on visual vocabularies of charity, benevolence and generosity.

> Two "totems" that have symbolized the humanitarian dyad of the victim and the relief worker

At the centre of these representations are two "totems"[1] that have symbolized the humanitarian dyad of the victim and the relief worker since the 19th century. That dyad is a visual convention,[2] a scene or figure employed frequently and widely over time and with which the public associates a specific meaning and affective connotation. This scenography, which is now iconic in humanitarian action, illustrates a hierarchization of these meaning-bearing figures. At the top is the aid worker, who acts as a necessary intermediary with whom the public can identify and who establishes the stability and effectiveness of aid around the world and over time. Though the figure of the male health worker has been imbued with heroic qualities, often featuring in humanitarian photography and cinema to exemplify self-sacrifice and courage, women are also very present in Red Cross posters.

The female nurse clearly evokes traditional figures of mercy and charity in religious iconography, particularly in Christian societies where such cultural referents occurred frequently at the turn of the 20th century. Visual evidence of this heritage abounds in the posters of 1914 to 1940, not only in the uniforms of Red Cross nurses, directly inspired by nuns' habits, but also in allegorical forms. There are myriad representations of the nurse as a pietà, among which the most famous is "The Greatest Mother in the World", drawn by Alonzo Foringer in 1918 for the American Red Cross. Since then, countless posters have featured mater dolorosa comforting wounded soldiers or unfolding her cloak or wings, suggesting a guardian angel who protects the vulnerable (see p. 45).

The counterpart to the aid worker is the aid beneficiary, whose image has evolved over time with the changing loci of humanitarian action and the development of international humanitarian law (IHL). The posters logically follow these evolutions to feature the categories of people receiving aid, illustrating the

[1] S. Sontag, *Regarding the Pain of Others*, Farrar, Straus and Giroux, New York, 2003.

[2] S. de Laat and V. Gorin, "Iconographies of humanitarian aid in Africa", *HPG Working Paper*, October 2016, pp. 15–30.

widening protections accorded initially to combatants and then to non-combatants. The first posters concentrate on the figure of the soldier, with the aim of minimizing the military aspect in order to emphasize the soldier's right to humane treatment. His uniform, which distinguishes the combatant from the non-combatant under IHL, is always recognizable, but it is his suffering that is in the foreground. His inability to fight is accentuated by his frequently vulnerable posture: he is prostrate, wounded and unarmed, creating an opening for humanitarian action. The 1920s mark a transition – a recognition that humanitarian activities were turning into permanent aid, in times of peace as in times of war. The posters bear witness to the appearance of new beneficiaries: images of wounded soldiers, often amputees, remained – reminding societies still scarred by fighting of the immense needs of those left disabled and prisoners of war – but next to them appeared civilians, often families. Children were figured with increasing frequency in the 1930s and 1940s; they represented a form of complete innocence while simultaneously underlining the Red Cross's new areas of activity, such as protecting youth and family ties, promoting health and nutrition, and aiding refugees and people with disabilities.

> A recognition that humanitarian activities were turning into permanent aid, in times of peace as in times of war

During the First World War, the humanitarian poster veered toward the realm of patriotic propaganda, revealing where it abutted the political, to such an extent that one could even call it "militarized charity".[3] The depoliticization of the Red Cross message – the neutrality of the victim reinforced by the iconography of suffering and relief – could not completely obscure the political dimension of the action from the moment that National Societies became army auxiliaries.[4] The combination of visual and textual rhetoric underscores the demands made of the civilian population to participate in the war effort, as in the Swiss poster created by Jules Courvoisier in 1917, in which the allegorical figure Helvetia, personifying Switzerland, is seated next to a Red Cross nurse (see p. 38). Calls for donations and for volunteers, young and old, emphasize mobilizing civilians. The posters use pleas, emotional appeals and moral pressure, such as "Do you have your Red Cross flag?", "Give!", "Think of the wounded" and "Join!".[5] The posters' visuals also bear witness to gradual changes in society. The posters of the 1940s and 1950s show female nurses in garb evoking army fatigues, an indication of how women achieved relative emancipation through work – and a foil to the female soldier. Red Cross Youth campaigns promoted the ideal of the youth volunteer by borrowing freely from the Scout movement, an image that contrasted with that of children in danger.

This blend of patriotism and nationalism, with the frequent presence of national flags, persisted through the Second World War.

[3] J. Hutchinson, *Champions of Charity: War and the Rise of the Red Cross*, Westview Press, Boulder, 1996.

[4] J. Horne, "'Neutrality-Humanity': The humanitarian mission and the films of the American Red Cross", in M. Braun et al. (eds), *Beyond the Screen: Institutions, Networks and Publics of Early Cinema*, Indiana University Press, Bloomington, 2012, pp. 11–18.

[5] G. Manno, "L'appel à l'aide humanitaire: un genre directif émotionnel", in *Les Émotions dans les Interactions*, C. Plantin et al. (eds), Presses Universitaires de Lyon, Lyon, 2000, pp. 279–94.

Afterwards, it evolved in a subtler direction: elements of folklore were employed, such as the Spanish flag day (1956), the Mongolian camel (1960) or the Belgian character Tintin created by the Hergé Foundation (1984). Posters for blood drives framed donation as a civic duty. For National Societies in socialist countries, images of the nurse and the Red Cross worker changed to adopt the new communist aesthetic of the proletariat figure: the male worker as a bare-chested, muscular man and the female kolkhoz farmer with her knotted scarf. This model – equally recognizable in Albanian, Uzbek, Polish, Russian, Chinese, Korean and Ugandan posters – transected cultures, and its call for collective effort paralleled those made in agriculture and industry.

While the Second World War did not engender any real rupture in visual conventions, the 1950s witnessed many significant shifts. As many humanitarian non-governmental organizations appeared, competition to assert the organizations' visual identities and missions accelerated. Posters about relief activities in the case of natural catastrophes from the International Federation of Red Cross and Red Crescent Societies (IFRC) and National Societies focus on preparation and reconstruction work. The creation of the United Nations system in this period also influenced the ideological framework of humanitarian action. In a world that would henceforth be marked by multilateral diplomacy and collective peace, nations had to engage in dialogue. At the same time, the world had bifurcated into the East-West axis of the Cold War. This provided the impetus for the ICRC to reaffirm its fundamental principles with the publication of jurist Jean Pictet's book on the subject in 1955. The new ideals were given visual form with new

symbols: hands extended between peoples, and a world illuminated by the promotion of such values as security, solidarity and universality (see p. 26). They were reminiscent of the humanist and altruistic values that gave rise to humanitarian sentiment in the 18th and 19th centuries. With the wave of decolonization wars in Asia and Africa, new nations were entering the international stage and wished to demonstrate their adhesion to the principles of goodwill underpinning the international community. Following the creation of new National Societies from the 1950s to 1970s, numerous posters evidenced the reappropriation of the principles of humanity and solidarity using the emblems of the Red Cross, Red Crescent and Red Lion and Sun[6], which created a kind of standardization. The most recent example of this is the 2017 poster from the South Sudan Red Cross Society, which was formed in June 2013.

As with any cultural product, the posters depend on the circumstances and sensibilities of their times, and their colonial dimension must be examined. The relationship between colonizing powers and indigenous peoples is evident in posters by National Societies created in areas under colonial administration, such as the Belgian Congo (see p. 17). The central position of the white doctor references advances in tropical medicine through the so-called bush doctors, who became a widespread figure starting in the late 1800s. Taking broad inspiration from the visual vocabulary of missionaries', voyagers' and explorers' photography, who captured exotic landscapes

[6] The Red Lion and Sun was recognized as an emblem by the ICRC in 1929 at the request of Iran, but ceased to be used following the Iranian Revolution in 1979.

while also presenting an encounter with the figure of the Other[7], the posters are an act of hierarchization. But they are equally an act of communication. Congolese Red Cross workers copied the work of the white doctor, marking a form of aid localization even in that early period.

One can also see this in the globalization of health-care and education policies launched since 1945, driven by UN agencies like the World Health Organization, the UN Refugee Agency and UNICEF. Practices diversified as they were adapted to sociocultural realities, which is particularly evident in national and international campaigns about hygiene, nutrition, disease and physical activity from the 1940s to 1960s. Communication via poster thus acquired a pedagogical dimension, seeking to promote good habits with particularly vulnerable segments of the population – whence a proliferation of posters aimed at children, with simple educational messages such as "Brush your teeth", or posters focused on women's family responsibilities. The tendency persisted through the following decades, reflecting National Societies' community social or health-care work, particularly with people suffering from social exclusion linked to age, poverty, addiction or xenophobia.

The relationship with a more or less geographically distant Other is symbolically treated[8] in post-colonial-era posters, which began to address North-South relationships starting in the 1960s. In European National Societies'

> These posters also challenge the perception of brutality and its representation by avoiding explicit violence

posters, the figure of the homegrown beneficiary was supplanted by images of African or Asian people. The visual politics of these posters underlines compassion towards distant populations, while at the same time essentializing and universalizing the figure of the Victim in now-archetypal contexts: famine, war and poverty[9]. The posters also reflect changes in the visual strategies of the ICRC, the IFRC and the National Societies, which reinforced their partnerships with television and photojournalism professionals in the 1950s.[10] Drawing thus gave way to photography in some posters, which evoke iconic images that had appeared in the international press, such as those of the Biafran famine of 1968 and of the Vietnamese boat people at the end of the 1970s.

Finally, these posters also challenge the perception of brutality and its representation by avoiding explicit violence. They operate by allusion, as with the shotgun shell referring to security problems in a New Zealand poster from 1999, or by euphemism, as with the drawing representing the Geneva Conventions, created by the artist Heinz-Jürgen Kristahn for the German Red Cross in the 1980s. Fear is employed much more effectively to raise awareness and change behaviour when evoked by unsettling symbols rather than by direct confrontation with images of death and destruction. The use of fear in the posters

[7] J. Lydon, *Photography, Humanitarianism, Empire*, Bloomsbury, London, 2016.

[8] L. Boltanski, *La Souffrance à Distance: Morale Humanitaire, Médias et Politique*, Métailié, Paris, 1993.

[9] N. Dogra, *Representations of Global Poverty: Aid, Development and International NGOs*, I.B. Tauris, New York, 2012.

[10] Y. Lavoinne, *L'Humanitaire et les Médias*, Presses Universitaires de Lyon, Lyon, 2002.

endures over time, whether it is through the monstrous, disease-spreading insects of the public health campaigns of the 1940s and 1950s, or the skeletons from the fights against smoking and AIDS in the 1980s and 1990s. The posters also decry the menace of deadly weapons, as in the campaign to ban anti-personnel mines launched after the Ottawa Treaty was signed in 1997, and the dangers of nuclear weapons, as with the mushroom cloud from the 2018 Marshall Islands poster. The posters thus convey the Red Cross's idealized vision for the world, where violence is encountered but swiftly supplanted by corrective action. It is a quality unique to the humanitarian narrative developed since the 18th century:[11] it does not deny the suffering of the body and the spirit – which is necessary to appeal to sentiment and justify action – yet it fosters hope.

[11] T. Laqueur, "Bodies, details, and the humanitarian narrative", in L. Hunt (ed.), *The New Cultural History*, University of California Press, Berkeley, 1989, pp. 176–204.

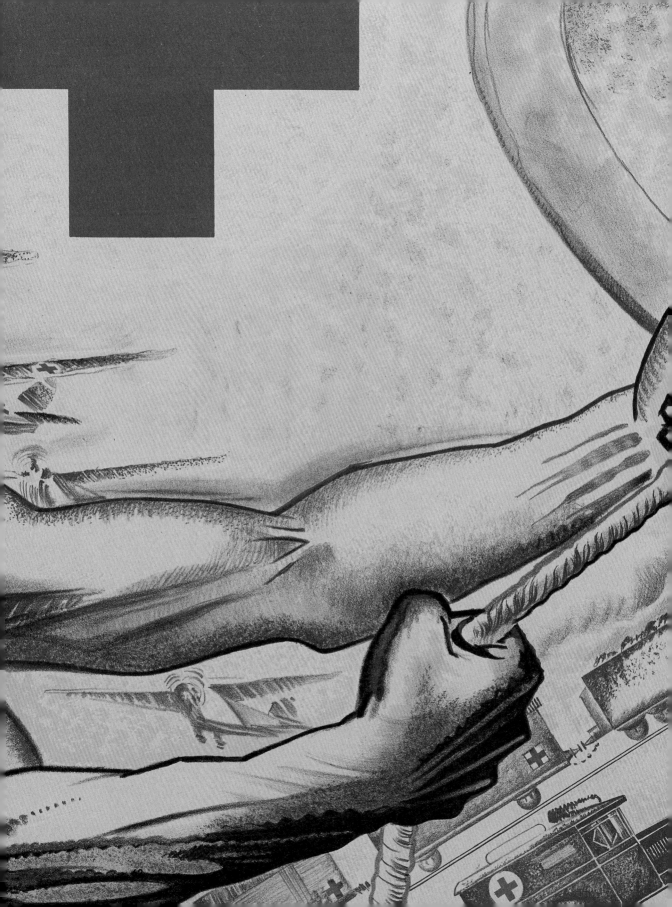

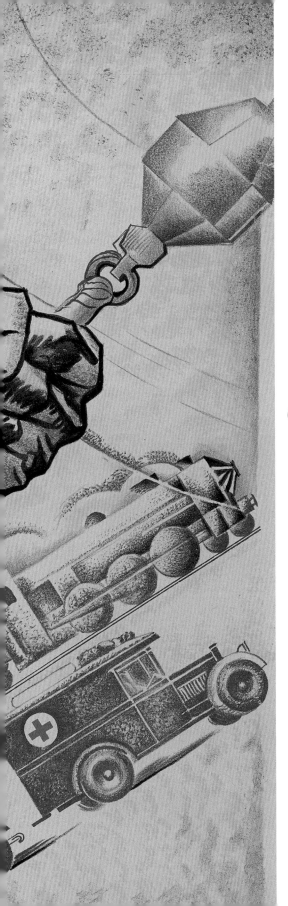

3

"On the job"

Unknown
Young first-aiders are always ready
Germany (former GDR), 1954
58.50 x 41 cm
MICR/BBT-2003-30-72

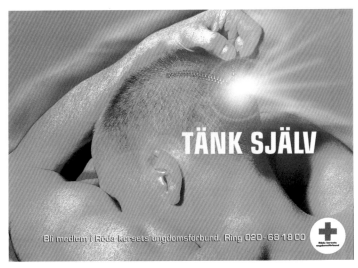

Walter Beach Humphrey
Builders of a new world
USA, n.d.
56 x 39 cm
MICR/BBT-2003-60-1

Unknown
Our schools serve our world
Nigeria, 1966
51 x 76 cm
MICR/BBT-2007-2-24

Patricia Dunlop
*In every country
the International Junior
Red Cross serves*
New Zealand, 1945
50 x 32 cm
MICR/BBT-2000-99-41

Horyd →
*Let's awaken hearts, let's
combine efforts, to work for
the Polish Red Cross*
Poland, 1934
100 x 68 cm
MICR/BBT-1986-28-213

Bogdan Nowakowski
*Together! Polish Red Cross
Youth Circle*
Poland, n.d.
70 x 54 cm
MICR/BBT-1986-28-227

N. Joukov, V. Klimashin, P. Piskounov
*Go, comrade, into battle.
Go, and be calm. I'm with you
everywhere. I'm coming,
comrade-warrior. You'll be hit
by lead, you'll be hit by shells,
but I'll be with you through all
your suffering*
Russian Federation (former USSR),
1943
29 x 39.5 cm
MICR/BBT-1988-4-1

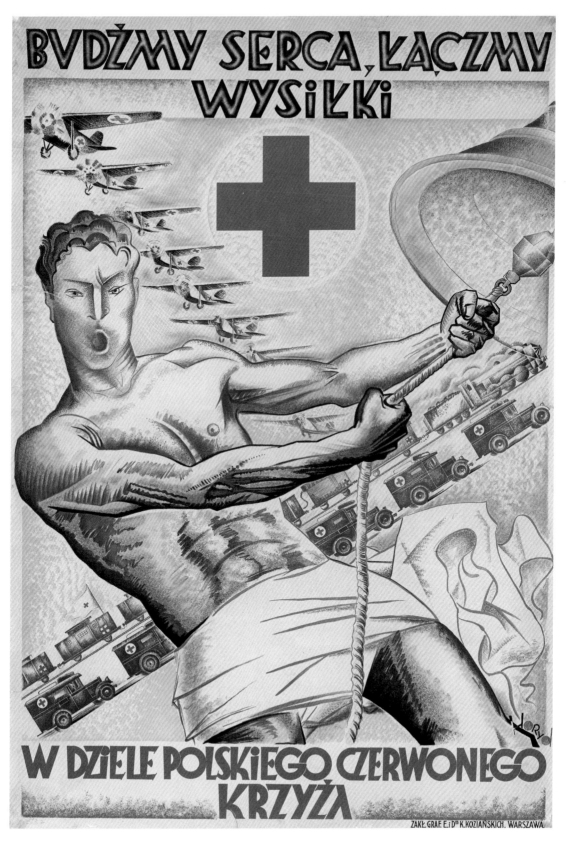

적십자 열성분자들이여!
대중적 위생훈련에 적극참가하자!

République de Corée

Unknown
*Enthusiastic members
of the Red Cross! Take an
active part in public health
promotion!*
Democratic People's
Republic of Korea, 1956
80 x 55 cm
MICR/BBT-1987-34-86

Unknown →
*Strong first aid services ensure
the smooth advancement of
production and construction*
People's Republic of China,
1955
76 x 52 cm
MICR/BBT-2001-18-32

搞好衛生急救，保証生産建設的順利進行

加急救訓練
積極爲生産服務

中國紅十字會上海市分會業

Viktor Koretsky, Vera Gitsevich,
E. Polotskaja
*Join the women's volunteer brigade
at the front. A first aider is a soldier's
best helper and friend!*
Russian Federation (former USSR), 1941
60 x 87.5 cm
MICR/BBT-1988-4-12

Gould
On the job
USA, 1956
48.5 x 38.5 cm
MICR/BBT-2000-218-51

Aljanvic Publicité
*Serve by becoming drivers
for the French Red Cross*
France, n.d.
65 x 50 cm
MICR/BBT-2001-18-31

Unknown
*Help those in need and give
generously during disasters –
help the Red Cross*
Tanzania (former Tanganyika), n.d.
47.5 x 34.5
MICR/BBT-2001-53-7

BE A RED CROSS VOLUNTEER

Publication of Uganda Red Cross Society
Printed in USSR at the order of the Soviet Red Cross

Unknown
Be a Red Cross volunteer
Uganda, n.d.
56 x 43 cm
MICR/BBT-2005-4-13

Unknown
Join
Australia, 1939-1945
100 x 66 cm
MICR/BBT-2003-42-11

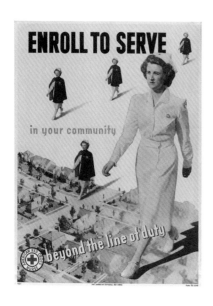

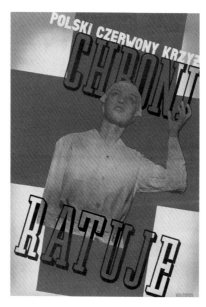

Unknown
Enroll to serve
USA, 1956
56.5 x 41 cm
MICR/BBT-2000-218-56

Unknown
*The Polish Red Cross protects
and saves lives*
Poland, 1935
101 x 69 cm
MICR/BBT-2004-1-11

J. Bernard Gyedes, Bertrand (Iramos)
The Red Cross is calling on you
Portugal, 1957
52 x 43 cm
MICR/BBT-2007-1-70

Henry Le Monnier
*The French Red Cross trains hospital nurses, social
workers and socio-medical aides – Learn more:
conditions of admission, study programmes*
France, n.d.
150 x 100 cm
MICR/BBT-2001-40-21

Unknown
Canadian Red Cross
Canada, 1914–1918
76 x 50 cm
MICR/BBT-1994-66-3

Unknown
Service – aid
Czech Republic, n.d.
57 x 41 cm
MICR/BBT-2005-10-58

Unknown
*3 million Koreans – let us all be members
of the Red Cross*
Republic of Korea, 1950–1953
77.5 x 51.5 cm
MICR/BBT-2001-53-60

Unknown
You too can help the Red Cross serve – join
France, n.d.
51 x 40 cm
MICR/BBT-2006-23-97

Joyce Dennys
VAD [Voluntary Aid Detachment]
United Kingdom, 1914–1918
75.5 x 50.5 cm
MICR/BBT-1986-28-254

Ruskin Williams
Join
Australia, 1939–1945
27 x 21 cm
MICR/BBT-2001-20-92

Howard Chandler Christy
The spirit of America
USA, 1919
76 x 51 cm
MICR/BBT-1987-91-9

Lawrence Wilbur
Join! The greatest mother
USA, 1930
76 x 51 cm
MICR/BBT-1987-91-4

Unknown
Hurry! The Red Cross needs you
United Kingdom, n.d.
73 x 49 cm
MICR/BBT-2001-7-34

Igbinogun, Amaeflinah
Ready, willing, able and glad to serve
Nigeria, 1955–1980
76 x 51 cm
MICR/BBT-2003-21-47

КЗЫЛ ЖАРИМАЙ ШӨЛКЕМИНЕ АҒЗА БОЛЫҢЛАР!

ВСТУПАЙТЕ В ЧЛЕНЫ ОБЩЕСТВА КРАСНОГО ПОЛУМЕСЯЦА!

D. Makhotin
*Become a member
of the Red Crescent
Society*
Uzbekistan
(former USSR), 1961
90.5 x 60 cm
MICR/BBT-2007-18-75

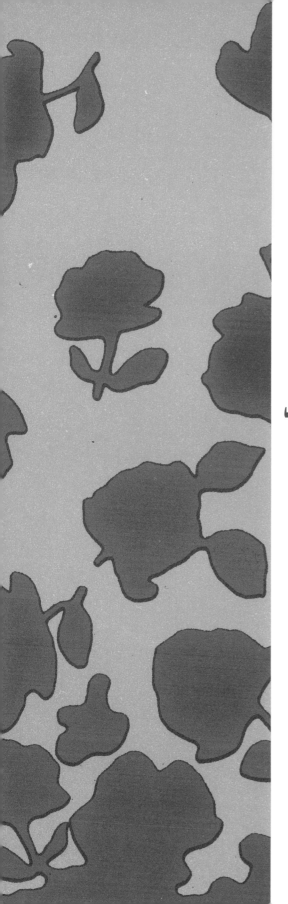

4

"Blood is life"

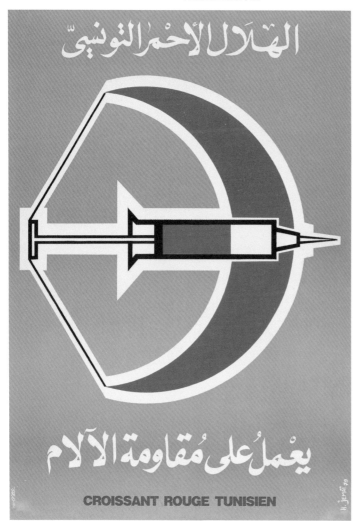

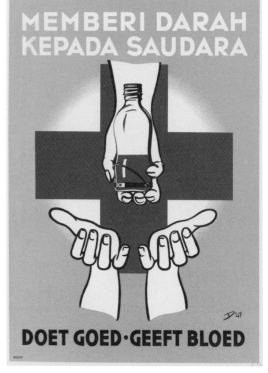

EGYPTIAN RED CRESCENT

جمعية الهلال الأحمر المصري

التبرع بالدم
واجب وطني
وإنساني

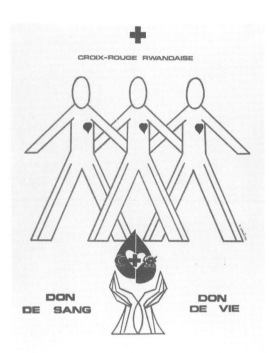

D. Lemaître
Rwandan Red Cross –
Give blood, give life
Rwanda, n.d.
40 x 30 cm
MICR/BBT-2002-7-2

Unknown
Wanted: you!
Finland, 1992
42 x 30 cm
MICR/BBT-2010-32-63

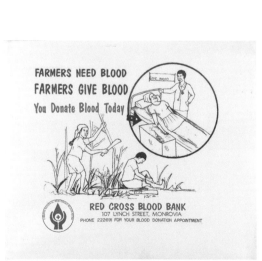

Unknown
Farmers need blood
Liberia, n.d.
35.5 x 43 cm
MICR/BBT-2002-29-66

BE A PROUD GIVER

DONATE BLOOD!

DATE: ....

VENUE: ....

DATE: ....

VENUE: ....

DATE: ....

VENUE: ....

ISSUED BY THE BOTSWANA RED CROSS SOCIETY

Unknown
Be a proud giver
Botswana, 1993
42 x 29.5 cm
MICR/BBT-2010-32-10

ALL MANKIND IS BOUND TOGETHER
BY A THIN RED LINE.

GIVE BLOOD...SAVE LIFE

Fiji Red Cross Society.

Unknown
Give blood... save life
Fiji, 1978
38.5 x 55.5 cm
MICR/BBT-2007-18-46

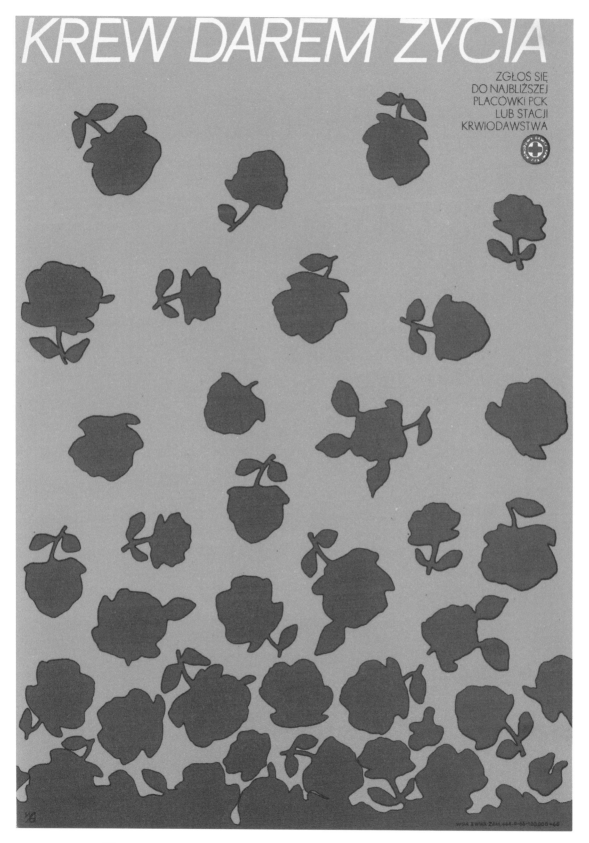

KREW DAREM ŻYCIA

ZGŁOŚ SIĘ
DO NAJBLIŻSZEJ
PLACÓWKI PCK
LUB STACJI
KRWIODAWSTWA

КРОВЬ — ЖИЗНЬ

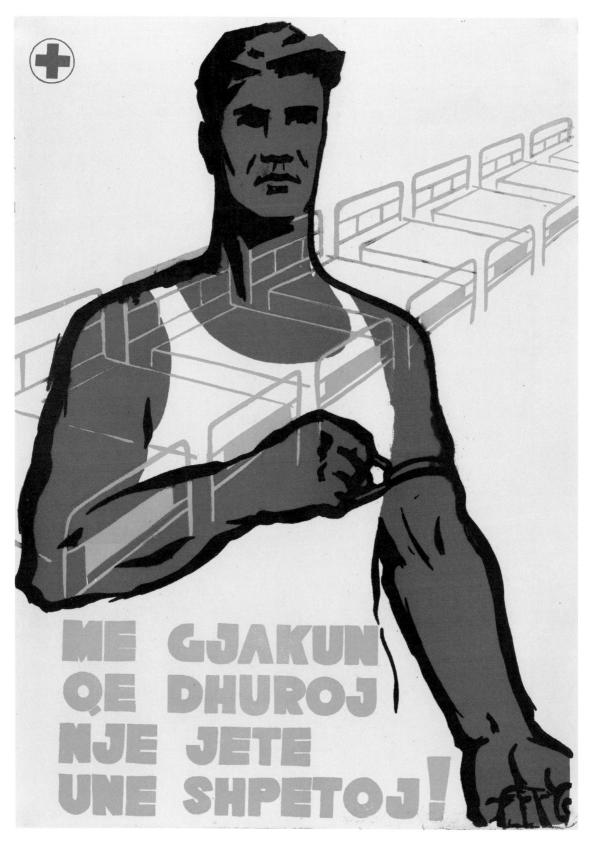

ME GJAKUN
QE DHUROJ
NJE JETE
UNE SHPETOJ!

← Unknown
*I save a life with the blood
that I give!*
Albania, n.d.
48 x 34 cm
MICR/BBT-2004-18-27

Unknown
*Become a blood donor
and save a life*
Zambia, 1978
76 x 49.5 cm
MICR/BBT-2001-118-70

E.I. Vladimirov
*In 20 years, I've given
40 litres of blood, and
I'm still in good health.
Why aren't you a donor?*
Uzbekistan (former USSR),
1965
50.5 x 34 cm
MICR/BBT-2005-34-16

Unknown
Give blood to save life
Papua New Guinea, n.d.
27.5 x 31 cm
MICR/BBT-1988-69-6

Unknown →
Become a donor
on the blood bus
Australia, 1973
43.5 x 28 cm
MICR/BBT-1989-51-14

PAPUA NEW GUINEA RED CROSS BLOOD TRANSFUSION SERVICE

P.O. Box 1174   Boroko   Telephone: 25 5753 / 24 8332   Telex: NE 23292

Also at: Alotau, Arawa, Goroka, Kavieng, Kimbe, Kundiawa, Lae, Madang, Mendi, Mount Hagen, Popondetta, Rabaul and Wewak.

Prize-winning design by ANDREW NUMBASA, Badihagwa High School.

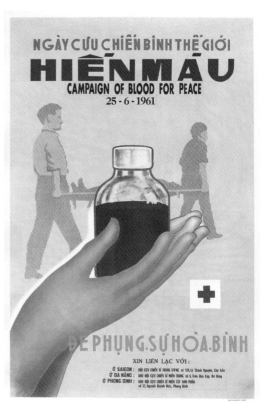

Unknown
Campaign of blood for peace
Vietnam, 1961
89 x 59 cm
MICR/BBT-2006-33-53

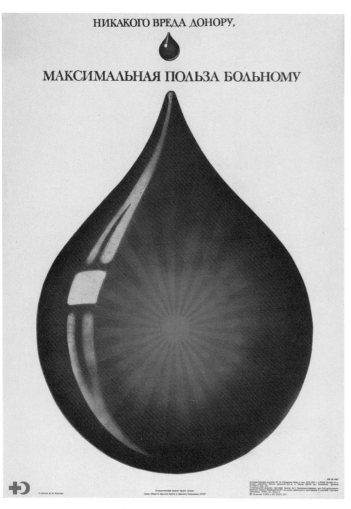

D.L. Kassil
No pain for the donor,
maximum benefit for the sufferer
Russian Federation
(former USSR), 1977
57 x 42 cm
MICR/BBT-2006-26-33

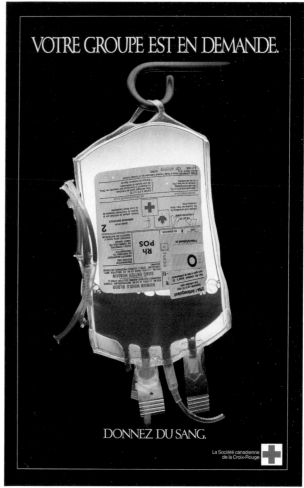

Unknown
*Your group is in demand.
Give blood.*
Canada, 1982
56 x 35.5 cm
MICR/BBT-2001-117-1

Unknown
*Blood supply is short again this summer.
Every summer and winter, there is a drop in
blood donors. The blood supply dries up, and
precious human life does, too. Register in our
blood donation booking system*
Japan, n.d.
73 x 51.5 cm
MICR/BBT-1989-51-19

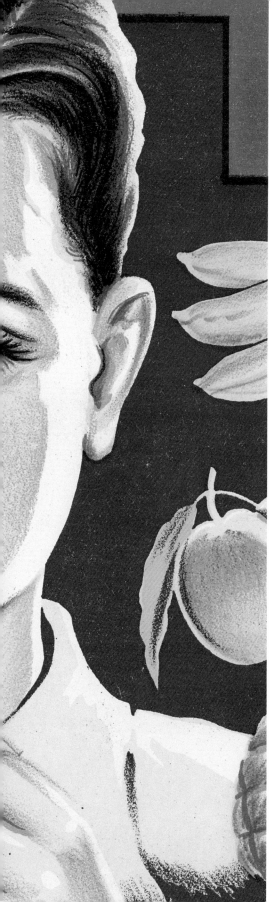

5

"We want to live healthy"

E.I. Paikov
Children with posture problems,
practice regular gymnastic exercise
Russian Federation (former USSR), 1965
43 x 29 cm
MICR/BBT-2005-10-97

P. Hazarie
Air, sun, water...that's health!
Romania, 1966
66 x 47 cm
MICR/BBT-2003-23-31

Karl Hauer
We want to live healthy –
good nutrition, exercise
and walks – serve, aid
Austria, n.d.
58.5 x 41 cm
MICR/BBT-2001-11-21

Unknown
For your health,
do morning exercises!
Bulgaria, 1969
69 x 47 cm
MICR/BBT-1999-154-9

за вашето
здраве
играйте
утринна
гимна -
стика !

← Jean Reid
Keep yourselves clean
South Africa, 1947
51 x 38 cm
MICR/BBT-2000-114-46

B. Sechiari
Keep your body clean
South Africa, 1947
51 x 38 cm
MICR/BBT-2000-114-37

WASH HANDS **BEFORE MEALS**

Published by THE JUNIOR RED CROSS , BRITISH RED CROSS SOCIETY, LONDON.S.W.I.

Levy
Wash hands before meals
United Kingdom, n.d.
43 x 37 cm
MICR/BBT-2000-99-51

Ullmann
Wash hands
South Africa, 1943
38 x 25.5 cm
MICR/BBT-2001-53-37

100

Clean Tips for food handlers

WASH HANDS

WITH SOAP AND WATER
BEFORE TOUCHING FOOD.
AFTER USING THE TOILET.
WHEN HANDS ARE SOILED.

ULLMANN

R L ESSON & CO LTD JOHANNESBURG   E/P 3/8/43
Published by the South African Red Cross Society, P.O. Box 8726, Johannesburg, and Approved by the Union Department of Public Health.

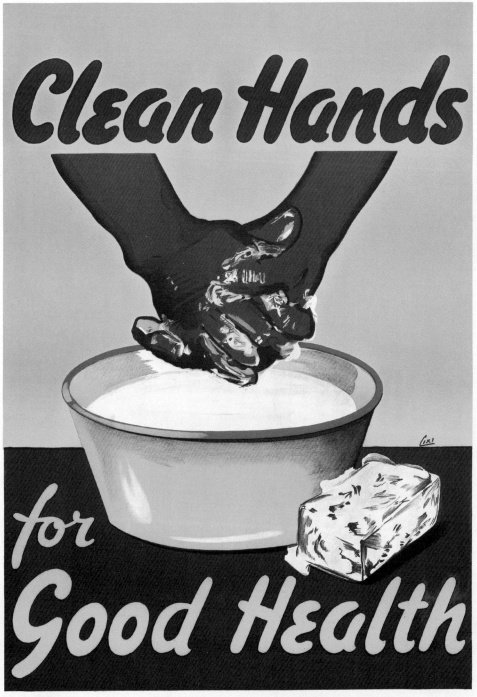

101

Vertil
Save your teeth
Belgium, n.d.
33.5 x 22 cm
MICR/BBT-2001-53-27

G. C.
*Clean your teeth night
& morning*
United Kingdom, n.d.
78 x 57 cm
MICR/BBT-2003-42-9

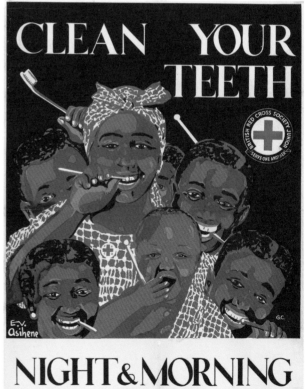

Kanuis
Danish Youth Red Cross
Denmark, n.d.
60.5 x 39.5 cm
MICR/BBT-2001-19-8

LAWS OF HEALTH

1 WASH HANDS ALWAYS BEFORE MEALS

2 BRUSH TEETH AND HAIR NIGHT AND MORNING

3 BREATHE THROUGH YOUR NOSE

4 WINDOWS OPEN NIGHT AND DAY

5 PLAY IN THE OPEN AIR AS MUCH AS YOU MAY

6 EARLY TO BED—10 HOURS SLEEP—& EARLY TO RISE

7 WASH ALL OVER WITH SOAP & WARM WATER AS OFTEN AS YOU CAN

JUNIOR RED CROSS

Unknown
Iraqi Red Crescent Society.
Sleep ten hours each night
for good health
Iraq, 1955
69 x 49.5 cm
MICR/BBT-2001-20-52

Unknown
Take a bath every day –
clean your teeth after food
Pakistan, 1956
51 x 38 cm
MICR/BBT-2000-99-60

TAKE A BATH EVERY DAY
CLEAN YOUR TEETH AFTER FOOD
هر روز غسل کیجئے ——— اپنے دانت کھانے کے بعد صاف کیجئے
PUBLISHED BY THE PAKISTAN RED CROSS SOCIETY, NATIONAL HEADQUARTERS, KARACHI

← P.J. Clement Johnston
Laws of health
United Kingdom, 1924
71.50 x 49.50 cm
MICR/BBT-2003-21-89

*Always sleep with your
windows open*
Pakistan, n.d.
51 x 38 cm
MICR/BBT-2001-25-22

Monblin
*We want: mother's breast milk,
healthy parents, sun and fresh air,
dry sheets, clean beds, regular
feeding, protection from flies –
Polish Red Cross – published
with Health Ministry approval*
Poland, 1943
85 x 55 cm
MICR/BBT-1986-28-209

Unknown
Keep baby clean
South Africa, 1946
50.5 x 38 cm
MICR/BBT-2001-25-15

Unknown
*Give children appropriate food
only – do not feed them unusual
or unhealthy food*
Myanmar (former Burma), n.d.
73.5 x 94 cm
MICR/BBT-2001-20-16

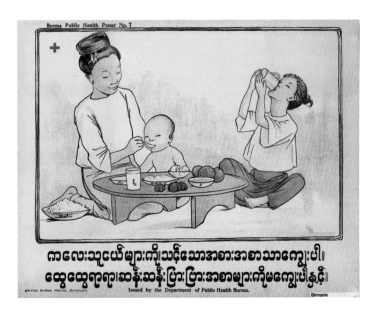

MINISTERE DE L'AGRICULTURE

buvez du
BON
LAIT

CROIX-ROUGE DE BELGIQUE ✚ CROISADE NATIONALE DE SANTE

Alcover
*Drink good milk – Ministry
of Agriculture*
Belgium, 1953
120 x 80 cm
MICR/BBT-2002-24-11

← Alcover
*Drink good milk – Ministry
of Agriculture*
Belgium, 1953
120 x 80 cm
MICR/BBT-2002-24-11

Adrian Watts
Keep goats
Australia, 1952
49.5 x 37 cm
MICR/BBT-1999-154-3

B. Sechiari
Good friends
South Africa, 1946
51.5 x 38 cm
MICR/BBT-2000-114-39

Published by THE PAKISTAN RED CROSS SOCIETY, NATIONAL HEADQUARTERS, KARACHI.

6

"Protect
yourself"

Unknown
(Untitled)
Canada, n.d.
24 x 43.5 cm
MICR/BBT-2006-22-47

Unknown
Coughing spreads germs –
cover your face when you cough
India, n.d.
47.5 x 35 cm
MICR/BBT-2003-23-85

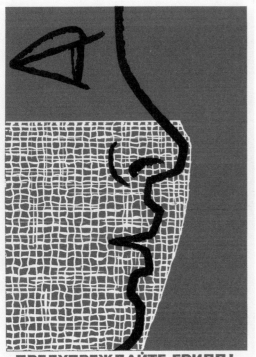

V. V. Kirev
Beware of flu
Ukraine (former USSR), 1977
43.5 x 29.5 cm
MICR/BBT-2005-29-33

K. Sakai
Japanese Red Cross Society – Let us cover our mouth and nose whenever sneezing or coughing
Japan, 1925
78 x 51 cm
MICR/BBT-1986-28-151

日本赤十字社

Let us cover our MOUTH and NOSE whenever sneezing or coughing.

咳やくしやみをするときは口鼻をおさへませう

JAPAN RED CROSS SOCIETY

Unknown
BCG – Tuberculosis Control Week
Former Yugoslavia, 1949
100.5 x 71 cm
MICR/BBT-2001-20-19

Unknown
Murder by carelessness!
Ireland, n.d.
15 x 49.5 cm
MICR/BBT-2005-29-26

B. Cascella
*Italians, help
the Red Cross in assisting
tuberculosis patients*
Italy, 1920
96.5 x 66.5 cm
MICR/BBT-2001-57-54

Ullman →
*Spitting is dangerous –
if you have tuberculosis,
always use a spittoon*
South Africa, 1952
78.5 x 52.5 cm
MICR/BBT-2001-25-89

SPOEG IS GEVAARLIK

SPOEG ALTYD IN 'N BAKKIE AS U AAN TERING LY

UITGEGEE DEUR DIE SUID-AFRIKAANSE ROOIKRUISVERENIGING
EN GOEDGEKEUR DEUR DIE UNIE-DEPARTEMENT VAN VOLKSGESONDHEID

R L ESSON & CO LTD JOHANNESBURG   A/P 22.8/43

Unknown
How to use and maintain latrine –
do not use: corncobs, rocks,
coconut skins, leaves, paper –
add water before using latrine,
after using latrine, clean latrine after
Cambodia, n.d.
59 x 42 cm
MICR/BBT-2010-20-146

Unknown
How cholera spreads: open
defecation and vomiting in rivers
by infected individuals. Individuals
who drink water contaminated by
cholera contract the disease.
Children who swim in contaminated
water contract the disease.
If mothers fetch contaminated
drinking water, their children
contract the disease – Ethiopian
Red Cross Society
Ethiopia, n.d.
57 x 43.5 cm
MICR/BBT-2002-24-90

Unknown
Cholera. Prevention is
better than cure.
India, 1953
76.5 x 51 cm
MICR/BBT-2001-25-68

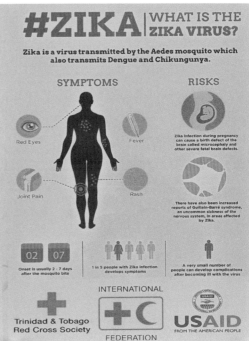

Unknown
#Zika – What is the Zika virus?
Trinidad and Tobago, 2017
28 x 21.5 cm
MICR/BBT-2018-1-5

Unknown
How to get rid of mosquitos that carry dengue – Mosquitos are vectors of dengue infection. Wash your water pot once a week, keep it covered, take your child to the health centre if you suspect dengue symptoms, check your waste basket and destroy any mosquito nests.
Cambodia, n.d.
60 x 42 cm
MICR/BBT-2010-20-145

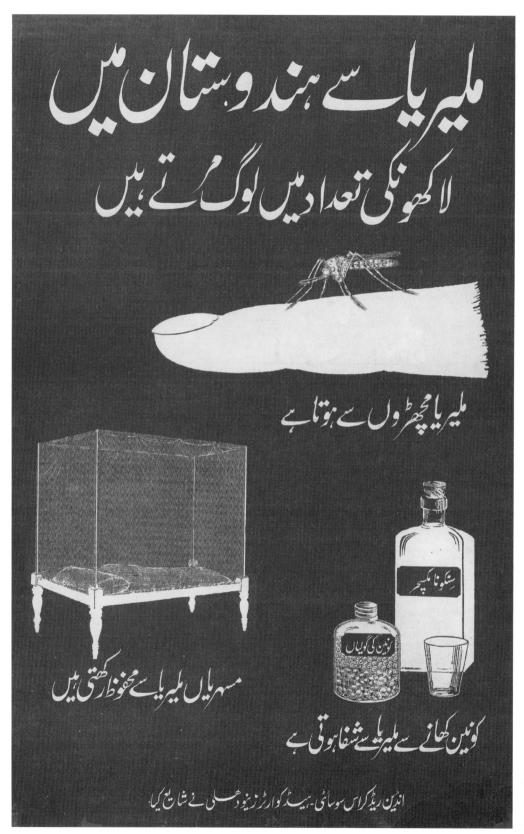

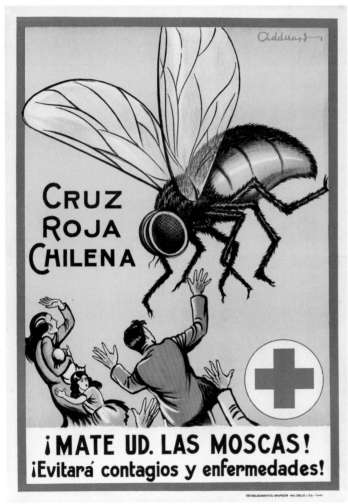

Unknown
Together against drugs
United Arab Emirates, 1990
70 x 51 cm
MICR/BBT-1997-34-1

Morris
To your health!
Belgium, 1987
60 x 42 cm
MICR/BBT-2002-30-67

Unknown
*Chewing coca leaves slows
your intelligence. Native Peruvians,
stop this vice that poisons your bodies*
Peru, n.d.
68 x 51.5 cm
MICR/BBT-2001-53-67

Unknown
Don't smoke
India, n.d.
76 x 50.5 cm
MICR/BBT-1999-154-14

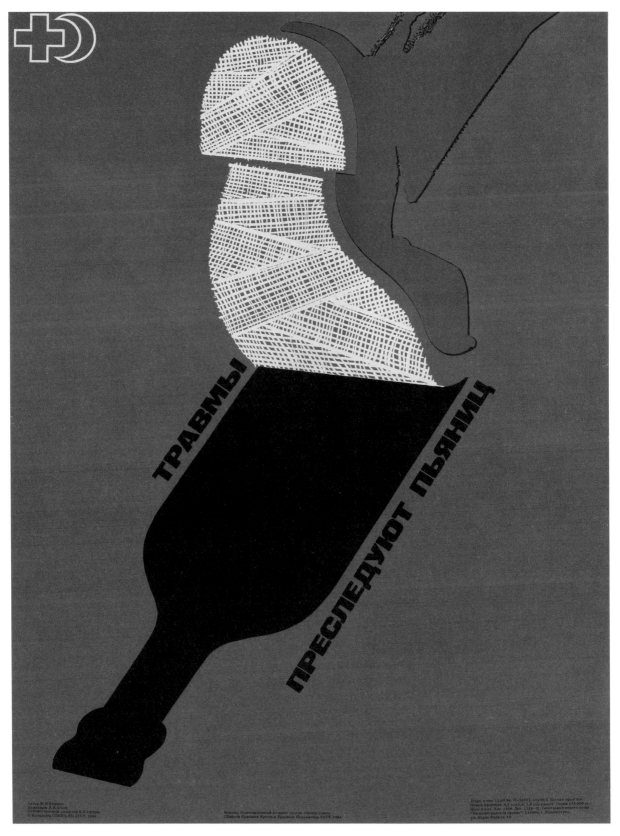

ТРАВМЫ ПРЕСЛЕДУЮТ ПЬЯНИЦ

Unknown
Open your eyes!
Look where you are going
South Africa, 1953
57.5 x 44.5 cm
MICR/BBT-2001-11-92

Ree Lordan
WOW!
South Africa, n.d.
57 x 44.5 cm
MICR/BBT-1987-34-107

Unknown
Prevent being blinded by welding torch
flash by wearing eye protection
South Africa, n.d.
58 x 45 cm
MICR/BBT-2001-18-26

← N. Berdin
Accidents follow alcoholics
Russian Federation (former USSR), 1986
58 x 43 cm
MICR/BBT-2002-30-54

Adra
What have you heard about HIV/AIDS?
Papua New Guinea, n.d.
42 x 30 cm
MICR/BBT-2010-20-60

U. Keele
The truth about AIDS. Pass it on...
China, n.d.
52 x 38 cm
MICR/BBT-2006-39-12

Martina Gobec →
Safe flight
Slovenia, 2000
98 x 68 cm
MICR/BBT-2010-20-5

Varen polet.

Univerza v Ljubljani, Akademija za likovno umetnost - Oddelek za oblikovanje, ilustracija in oblikovanje: Martina Gobec, 4. letnik, 2000, mentor: Peter Skalar, red. prof., izdal Rdeči križ Slovenije, 2000

Ustavimo AIDS!

Nobody has the truth written on their face.
Protect yourself.
Use a condom.

Trinidad & Tobago Red Cross Society

Unknown
Protect yourself
Trinidad and Tobago, 2017
61 x 46 cm
MICR/BBT-2018-1-1

INFORMATION - YOUR FIRST DEFENCE AGAINST

AIDS

ÖSTERREICHISCHES JUGENDROTKREUZ

HERAUSGEBER: ÖSTERREICHISCHES JUGENDROTKREUZ, GENERALSEKRETARIAT, WIEDNER HAUPTSTRASSE 32, A-1041 WIEN.   KONZEPT UND FOTO: CLAUDIO ALESSANDRI. MAKE UP UND FRISUREN: BRIGITTE AIGNER.   DRUCK: RASER, 1100 WIEN. GEDRUCKT AUF UMWELTFREUNDLICH HERGESTELLTEM PAPIER.

Claudio Alessandri
*Information – Your first
defence against AIDS*
Austria, 1998
60 x 84 cm
MICR/BBT-2000-83-8

ARCS

Unknown
*ARCS. Every year,
2.3 million people die from AIDS.
Since 1981, 25 million people have died*
Armenia, 2003
42 x 59 cm
MICR/BBT-2011-48-3

Unknown
No discrimination
Tunisia, 2017
42 x 30 cm
MICR/BBT-2017-37-4

Unknown
*Men play an important role
in fighting AIDS*
Syrian Arab Republic, n.d.
68 x 49 cm
MICR/BBT-2010-20-170

Unknown
Hispanic SIDA program
USA, n.d.
62 x 74 cm
MICR/BBT-1995-192-2-4

Posters and their images

Martin Heller

Posters are everywhere we look. That's what sets them apart from other media. Only when we start to see them not as works of art, but as images that convey a message, can we begin to grasp the sheer vastness of the genre.

A stub of paper nailed to a tree with a heart-rending photo of a missing cat? That's a poster. An imposing advertising display like an over-sized smartphone? That's a poster. A discount on oranges at your local supermarket? That's a poster. A lithographic print from the heyday of tourist advertising? That's a poster, too.

Diverse as they may be, posters have two things in common: they have a clear purpose, and they exist in numerous copies – never in isolation.

These observations lead us to a working definition of what a poster is: a universal, highly versatile medium with a long history and a barely comprehensible present. And that's precisely what makes posters so interesting – the fact that they serve a purpose, and that they seem to work. They're visually appealing, and they speak to people's needs and desires. And yet, despite what cognitive psychologists and market researchers would have us believe, exactly how they affect us remains largely a matter of speculation.

What's more, posters hold a special place in public life. They become a celebration of images for anyone willing and able to see this uncomplicated yet compelling set of symbols, stories, messages, invitations and inducements. And they compete mercilessly for our attention – among themselves, and with the myriad other sights and sounds that inhabit and shape our public spaces.

Thinking

I've chosen to introduce my thoughts about posters in this way because I've spent a large part of my working life thinking deeply about posters – as a graduate of the Basel School of Decorative Arts, as an art historian with a special interest in Pop Art, as someone who's commissioned works of art, as curator of the poster collection at the Museum für Gestaltung in Zurich, as a catalogue writer, and as a keen critic and observer of everyday life.

It is for that very reason that my thoughts below draw not on theory, but – and, I hope, more usefully – on my personal recollections and anecdotal accounts from a life spent working with posters. In any event, I make no claim to be a theorist. I'm merely a practitioner with a penchant for reflection.

Recently, while waiting for a train at Zurich Enge station, I spotted a man putting up a new poster on a large billboard on the other side of the track. With an elegance that almost seemed to belong to a different age, he unfurled each section, brushed on a layer of glue from his bucket, lined them up side by side, and smoothed them into place. Every move was made with the utmost precision – neither too much nor too little. The result was sheer perfection.

For a fleeting moment, that choreographed scene from everyday life unexpectedly stirred

A stub of paper nailed to a tree with a heart-rending photo of a missing cat? That's a poster

something inside me and caused me to forget I was looking at a piece of advertising. Tellingly, I drew a blank when, shortly afterwards, I tried to remember what the poster was about.

Collecting

My interest in posters goes back to my childhood. I was fascinated that something so simple could have such an impact, and at how they cost little to nothing. I was a particular admirer of Hans Falk's Expo 64 series. I was amazed that people could access art in that way. I naturally followed the poster of the year awards, which began in 1968. I was also a big fan of Swiss graphic artists at the time, for whom posters were about more than advertising. They were a medium for artistic expression.

Twenty years on, I was appointed curator of one the world's biggest poster collections, at the Museum für Gestaltung. I experienced first-hand the trials and tribulations of working as a museum curator. In addition to dealing with conservation matters, I also had to juggle the museum's collection policy. As well as making targeted acquisitions, we also received at least one copy of every poster put up in Switzerland from the ever-growing Société Générale d'Affichage (SGA) collection. Then I had to deal with replacing the museum's old A5 card-format catalogue with a new, easier-to-manage electronic version.

It was all new to me. For the first time, I was exposed to the world of collectors, with all their quirks, their special interests and their veiled rivalries. I came to learn about trading, about auctions, and about how the market obsesses with so-called "important"

posters – pieces of exceptional artistic merit in prime condition – and certain big names. And I discovered that experts fixate not on the medium itself, but instead on how a given poster performs in the market, as determined by its history or, indeed, its price.

The museum's collection, in all its depth and breadth, lent itself to numerous exhibitions and publications, many of which helped to foster a deeper understanding of what posters are and how they work.

Analysing

One particular exhibition, *Anschläge. Plakatsprache in Zürich: 1978–1988 (Posters/ Attacks. The Language of the Poster in Zurich: 1978–1988),*[1] was a real watershed moment – for two reasons. First, instead of celebrating the past, it was rooted firmly in the present. And second, it looked at the creative process as a form of interaction and rejection. Its focus was the ground-breaking and highly inventive visual language employed by Zurich's youth movement, which emerged amid the turbulence of the 1980s. That language became ever more radical as Zurich's young people took to the streets to demand space for the alternative arts scene, prompting riots and running battles in an otherwise conservative and orderly city. Images of the clashes were broadcast around the world.

Yet the youth movement's posters were simple in design. Most were calls to protest, invitations to parties and concerts, or political and social slogans. They can only be understood

---

[1] M. Heller and A. Marendaz (eds.), *Anschläge. Plakatsprache in Zürich: 1978–1988*, Museum für Gestaltung Zürich Catalogue (Doc. 368), Zurich, 1988. Museum für Gestaltung Zürich exhibition: 31 August – 23 October 1988.

against the backdrop of the city's official – and somewhat less polished – posters, and the culture from which they sprang. Art was the theatre of a cultural and social war between two visual worlds that could not have been further apart.

Although posters reflect reality, they shape it in a way that suits their purpose and their message

Eventually, the youth movement passed its peak. But it left behind a lasting legacy, as advertisers came to adopt many of the ground-breaking techniques employed in its posters. Tracking how advertising posters evolved over the years reveals how keen advertisers were to embrace these fresh ideas and use their creative muscle to keep pace with the changing times, no matter the cost.

The *Anschläge* exhibition clearly showed the extent to which posters "react" to the social conditions of the day, how, as weapons, they become part and parcel of those conditions, and how, eventually, those weapons become blunt.

Interpreting

The Swiss Confederation marked its 700th anniversary in 1991. But with the secret files scandal still fresh in people's minds, there was little appetite for celebration, and large swaths of Switzerland's cultural scene refused to honour the occasion. The stage was set perfectly for a tongue-in-cheek exhibition (we didn't have enough money for a publication), which we called *Schweizerwelt. Plakate aus der Sammlung (Swiss World. Posters from the Collection).*[2]

The exhibition posed a straightforward question: what if Switzerland were to disappear without a trace after 700 years, and what if the posters in the Museum's collection were the only surviving evidence that the country, and its people, had ever existed? What would that tell future generations about Switzerland?

The idea was to put the posters in the dock, to examine their content carefully, and to acknowledge, just this once, that the evidence might be misleading. The exhibition was akin to an ethnographic study, with chapters covering every aspect of Switzerland and its people. Why did it choose the cross as its national emblem? What were Swiss mothers like? What plants and animals lived there? What did its people eat and drink? What kind of relationship did it have with the rest of the world, as captured by the globe symbol? And so much more.

Inspired by the mountain trail layout employed at Expo 64, we arranged the posters in a line and let the content speak for itself. If the advertising posters for fuel, cocoa, toothpaste and soap were to be believed, Switzerland was a country inhabited not just by squirrels and foxes, but also by tigers, elephants, flamingos and other exotic creatures. The legendary William Tell, meanwhile, was seemingly so popular that he could wear a pair of Levi's jeans with his shepherd's cloak, and represent political views across the spectrum. And then there was the Swiss people's apparent reverence and affection for the globe – a symbol that played a bit-part role in everyday life but, in the cosmos, served as the backdrop for a chilled draught beer.

[2] Exhibition: *Schweizerwelt. Plakate aus der Sammlung.* Concept: Martin Heller. Museum für Gestaltung Zürich. 10 July – 25 August 1991.

There was, of course, a serious point to all this fun: although posters reflect reality, they shape it in a way that suits their purpose and their message. While that observation was nothing new, it was a salutary reminder that we need to apply filters whenever we're interpreting posters.

Judging

One of the highlights of my time at the Museum für Gestaltung was an exhibition entitled *Die 99 schlechtesten Plakate (The 99 Worst Posters).*[3] We wanted to take a swipe at the judging panels behind competitions like "The 100 Best Posters" in Switzerland, Germany, New Zealand, and elsewhere – to express our deep dissatisfaction with the process, and to rail against their opaque and perplexing award criteria. The experts know what makes something good, what makes it the best, but they give scant regard to how posters actually function.

"Some posters are good because others are bad. Good cannot exist without bad, and vice versa. They feed off and stimulate one another. That holds true in life, in art, and in design. And yet, for reasons we can understand, bad is often easier to grasp than good."

That statement of the obvious formed the opening lines of the exhibition guide for *Die 99 schlechtesten Plakate.*[4] The guide recounted the main arguments and conclusions of a lengthy discussion about what makes a poster – or rather, posters – good or bad. We dug deep into the collection, comparing and contrasting posters to try to work out what "bad" actually meant.

We set two rules from the outset.
The first rule was to exclude catalogued pieces from our search because, amid a flurry of new posters, they were the ones we had already identified as being important (and, therefore, "good") according to our standard selection criteria. The "bad" ones were put to one side – piles of posters measuring 90.5 × 128 cm, known in Switzerland as "World format" and elsewhere as "Swiss format". I was tasked with sifting through these vast piles of Swiss posters (the exhibition covered Swiss posters only). I examined each and every one in minute detail, smelling the ink, running my fingers over the paper, and developing the kind of physical relationship with them I'd never imagined could be possible.

The second rule was that I would be personally responsible for selecting the 99 worst posters because, when it comes to judging a work of art, there are no universal rules. It's largely a matter of personal taste. To my mind, acting as judge and jury on what was "bad" came at great personal risk.

My main takeaway from that exercise was that a poster can be bad for all sorts of reasons. A bad poster can fail to get its intended message across. It can be sexist or racist. It can be

[3] Exhibition: *Die 99 schlechtesten Plakate*. Concept: Martin Heller. Museum für Gestaltung Zürich. 23 November 1994 – 15 January 1995.

[4] M. Heller (ed.), *Prämiert weil jenseits. Die 99 schlechtesten Plakate*, Schule und Museum für Gestaltung Zürich, Vol. 14, Zurich, 1995, p. 44.

[5] B. Haldner (ed.), "Niklaus Stoecklin. 1896–1982", *Graphistes suisses*, Vol. 3, Museum für Gestaltung Basel, Basel, 1986. Museum für Gestaltung Zürich exhibition: 18 June – 13 August 1986.

[6] M. Heller (ed.), "Otto Baumberger. 1889–1961", *Graphistes suisses*, Vol. 4, Museum für Gestaltung Zürich, Zurich, 1988. Museum für Gestaltung Zürich exhibition: 26 May – 17 July 1988.

well-designed but dull. It can be ill-conceived. It can treat its audience like idiots. Or it can be well-meaning but naive. In other words, there are countless reasons why we might criticize a poster or question its impact, rationale, credibility or usefulness. But before we do so, we must recognize that posters, as easily accessible images that convey a message, are an inherently complex medium.

Championing a cause

In my time as a museum curator I have, of course, been involved in exhibitions and publications with a more historical slant, such as retrospectives of particular artists' work (like Niklaus Stoecklin[5] and Otto Baumberger[6]), posters from particular countries (such as Japan[7]), or specific genres such as film posters[8] (where pieces have to follow certain contextual rules to be recognized as belonging to that genre).

> Social and political posters speak primarily to human concerns

For me, there is one particular genre that stands head and shoulders above the rest for its sheer power and diversity: social and political posters, like those held in the International Red Cross and Red Crescent Museum collection.

Unlike advertising posters hawking consumer goods, low-cost fashion, tourist resorts or online platforms, social and political posters speak primarily to human concerns. How do we shine a light on abuse of power and the harm it causes? How can we depict mental and physical injuries without being voyeuristic? Do we have any credible images that convey a sense of hope and show people doing something to help? Can posters impart complex messages without resorting to cheap tricks and sensationalism?

Various events over the years have forced me to confront these questions. The Museum's collection supplied most of the pieces for exhibitions commemorating the Spanish Civil War[9] and the May 1968 uprising in Paris,[10] as well as a high-profile retrospective of Soviet propaganda posters.[11] Those historical posters conveyed a palpable immediacy that would simply be out of the question in today's world. They echoed a desire for social change, with the artists behind them using often ground-breaking visual language to further that cause. The genre, which we might term "art that speaks to the heart", carries a sense of necessity that commercial advertising simply cannot.

In 1997, the Museum für Gestaltung held an exhibition of Bruno Margadant's poster collection, entitled *Hoffnung und Widerstand. Das 20. Jahrhundert im Plakat der internationalen Arbeiter- und Friedensbewegung*

[7] C. Burer (ed.), *Kirei – Plakate aus Japan*, Museum für Gestaltung Zürich catalogue, Edition Stemmle, Schaffhausen, 1993. Museum für Gestaltung Zürich exhibition: 2 June – 31 July 1993.

[8] W. Beilenhoff and M. Heller (ed.), *Das Filmplakat*, Museum für Gestaltung Zürich catalogue, Scalo, Zurich/Berlin/New York, 1995. Museum für Gestaltung Zürich exhibition: 8 March – 30 April 1995.

[9] M. Heller (ed.), *Der Spanische Bürgerkrieg*, Museum für Gestaltung Zürich series, Vol. 5, Zurich, 1986. Museum für Gestaltung Zürich exhibition: 28 May – 7 September 1986.

[10] K. Meyer-Herzog, *Chiffre 68*, Höhere Schule für Gestaltung Zürich series, Vol. 9, Zurich, 1988. Museum für Gestaltung Zürich exhibition: *Im Mai. 1968 – Plakate aus Frankreich*. 19 May – 17 July 1988.

[11] V. B. Fedjuschin, M. Heller (eds.), *Kunst und Propaganda. Sowjetische Plakate bis 1953*, Museum für Gestaltung Zürich Catalogue (Doc. 371), Zurich, 1989. Museum für Gestaltung Zürich exhibition: 1 June – 13 August 1989.

[12] B. Margadant, *Hoffnung und Widerstand. Das 20. Jahrhundert im Plakat der internationalen Arbeiter- und Friedensbewegung*, Hans-Rudolf Lutz, Zurich, 1998. Museum für Gestaltung Zürich exhibition: 2 September – 18 October 1998.

(*Hope and Resistance. 20th-century Posters from the Workers' and Pacifist Movements*).[12] The exhibition, and the accompanying guide, provided a fascinating insight into that very sense of necessity. It showed the extent to which people's faith in a better world leaves political posters open to criticism for being too ambitious, overly simplistic and naive – at least in the eyes of those who don't share that same faith.

That said, a poster can only be judged in the context of its culture and its intended audience. Any conclusions we might draw from posters made in the 20th century – the time when Margadant was alive – have little to no relevance in today's globalized, media-dominated world. In the 21st century, political posters have taken on an entirely different meaning.

They are inseparable from the machinery of public relations, which shapes a large part of modern-day political discourse. These days, most of that debate happens online – to the extent that social networks and posters, in both the narrow and broad senses of the term, are as one.

We literally live in a different world, one that the Museum für Gestaltung recently explored through an exhibition entitled *Protest! Widerstand im Plakat (Protest! Resistance Posters)*.[13] The event looked at how images circulate in today's society, and how our complex relationships and dependencies shape the way that images are shared. The ensuing discussions raised plenty of new questions, and it became clear that there remains little value in treating posters in isolation, since they no longer reflect reality.

Winding down

I left the Museum für Gestaltung in 1998, thus bringing to an end a period of my life when I worked with posters on a daily basis. I went from being a devotee and expert to being a consumer. Nowadays, posters are merely some of the many objects I observe around me. That duty I once felt to understand them, to study them against uniform rules, has long gone. Yet that change of perspective is interesting in itself. It's what has allowed me, as I have done here, to share thoughts and observations gleaned from decades of experience, albeit anecdotally and haphazardly. Moreover, my occasional work for the Museum since then has further honed my understanding of the medium, and enabled me to see things in a different light.

I've learned what makes a poster – the interests, ambitions and opportunities behind it – and what determines its impact. I've met passionate, obsessive collectors, and I've seen how narrow-minded they can be. I've experienced how posters feel and what they smell like when they're hot off the press and as they age. I've seen how fragile they can become and learned how best to restore them. I've even picked up a few tips like how to put up a poster, and what glue to use, so there are no visible folds once it's dry, and how to get it looking as smooth and appealing as a baby's skin. These are very much my own thoughts about the themes I've come into contact with, the creative people I've met, their judgements and prejudices, how the medium is received, and the wider historical circumstances. All of

[13] B. Rogger, J. Voegeli, R. Widmer and Museum für Gestaltung Zürich (eds.), *Protest. Eine Zukunftspraxis*, Lars Müller Publishers, Zurich, 2018. Museum für Gestaltung Zürich exhibition (Toni Areal): *Protest! Widerstand im Plakat*. 20 April – 2 September 2018.

those things have shaped my understanding of, and my affection for, posters – as images that are tied to, and even depend on, the visual worlds of art and the everyday. Every time I see an interesting poster, I cannot help but wax lyrical about imagery.

These days, I'm happy being a mere fan of the genre. I'm an observer who appreciates a good poster but has other interests too. My feelings about posters are fluid. I enjoy having them around me at home, in social settings or when I'm visiting a cultural attraction. But sometimes I see them as just one of the many and increasingly complex – and effective – ways we're bombarded with messages from all sides. In that sense, they've become part of the background noise.

They've become
part of the background
noise

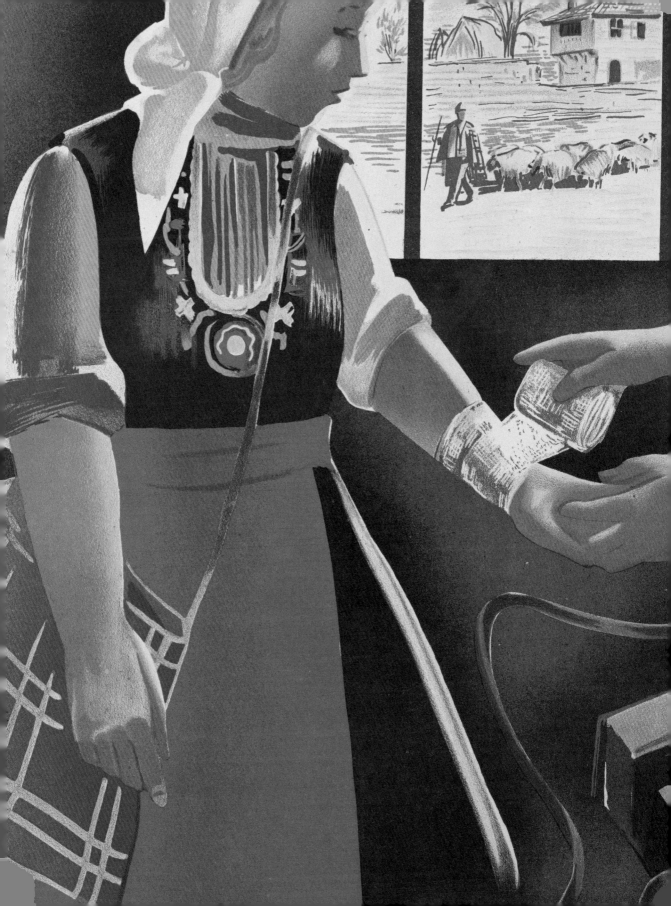

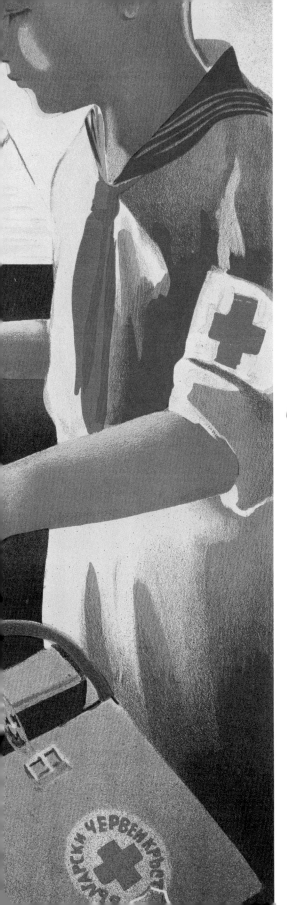

7

"Can you help?"

Unknown
*A touch of loyalty and gratitude
– Qatar Red Crescent Society*
Qatar, n.d.
50 x 35.5 cm
MICR/BBT-1995-123-12

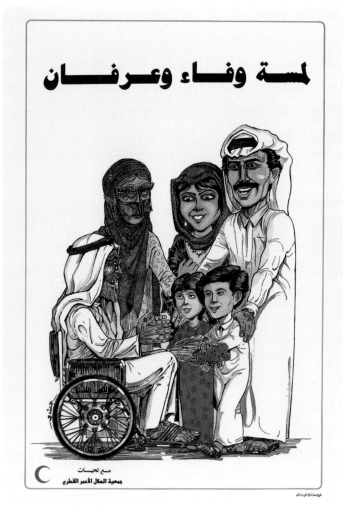

Unknown
*How to recognize and treat a stroke or
heart attack – What are the signs of heart
attack? What are the signs of stroke?*
Magen David Adom in Israel
Israel, 2015
70 x 50 cm
MICR/BBT-2016-3-2

Unknown
*Join the Red Crescent,
learn how to help!!!*
Somalia, 1964
61 x 46 cm
MICR/BBT-2001-54-65

Unknown
First Aid – You never know when you'll need it
New Zealand, n.d.
30 x 42 cm
MICR/BBT-1995-124-3

Unknown
Always ready – One for all
Germany, 2005
42 x 59.5 cm
MICR/BBT-2005-32-1

Unknown
Leadership & instructor training
USA, 1953
43.5 x 36 cm
MICR/BBT-2001-18-36

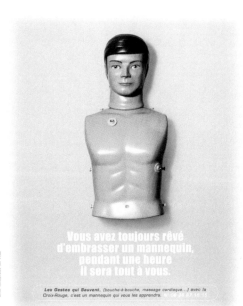

R. Truqueti
You've always dreamed of kissing a model, and for an hour, she's all yours. Learn life-saving techniques (mouth-to-mouth, CPR, etc.) with a model, and the Red Cross.
French Red Cross – We tolerate no suffering
France, 2000
40 x 30 cm
MICR/BBT-2001-21-6

Unknown
Volunteer at a women's shelter
Iceland, 2017
42 x 30 cm
MICR/BBT-2017-44-4

R. Truqueti
You've always dreamed of kissing a model, and for an hour, she's all yours. Learn life-saving techniques (mouth-to-mouth, CPR, etc.) with a model, and the Red Cross.
French Red Cross – We tolerate no suffering
France, 2000
40 x 30 cm
MICR/BBT-2001-21-7

Unknown
*Be ready for first aid – Children, take
first-aid classes*
Bulgaria, 1949
69 x 48.5 cm
MICR/BBT-2001-11-38

Unknown →
Learn to save others' lives
Ghana, n.d.
78 x 52 cm
MICR/BBT-1999-154-1

Unknown
Can you help?
USA, 1947
31 x 23.5 cm
MICR/BBT-2001-11-45

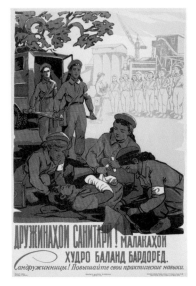

A. Matchigov
*Health team members!
Increase your skills*
Tajikistan (former USSR), 1962
80 x 54 cm
MICR/BBT-2005-34-24

Learn to save Others' Lives

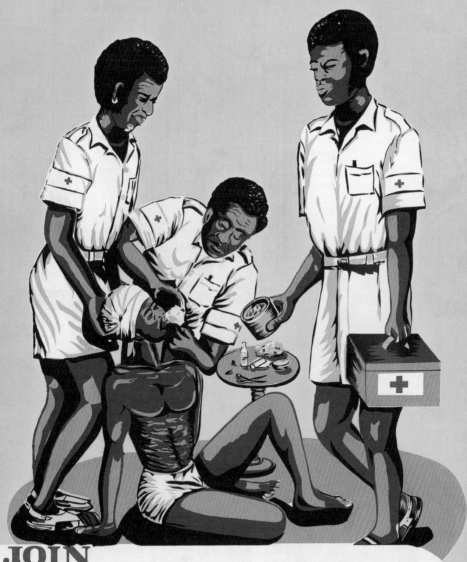

JOIN The RED+CROSS NOW

Unknown
Care for the elderly
Mongolia, n.d.
39.5 x 29.5 cm
MICR/BBT-1992-24-53

Jack Sey →
The elderly – We teach in-home health care
France, 1967
40 x 30 cm
MICR/BBT-2006-23-6

 ӨНДӨР НАСТНЫГ ХАЛАМЖЛАЯ

R. Muray
*Care more for the elderly,
provide serenity in old age*
Hungary, 1963
68.5 x 47.5 cm
MICR/BBT-2003-25-30

Unknown
*Help protect the indigent
from the indigent*
Afghanistan, n.d.
52.5 x 36 cm
MICR/BBT-2002-13-39

Unknown →
*I see what you don't see.
Poverty: don't look away –
Youth Red Cross*
Germany, 2009
42 x 30 cm
MICR/BBT-2011-1-4

Ich sehe was, was du nicht siehst.*

*Viele von uns haben in der Schule dauernd Probleme. Du kannst das nicht sehen, aber häufig liegt es daran, dass sie arm sind. Denn in Deutschland haben arme Jugendliche schon von Anfang an schlechte Karten – und fast jeder siebte ist davon betroffen. Was wir gemeinsam dagegen tun können, erfährst du beim Jugendrotkreuz: **www.schaunichtweg.de**

ARMUT: SCHAU NICHT WEG! JUGENDROTKREUZ

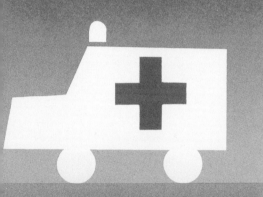

8

"Only one thing
stops the Red
Cross"

Tom Stoddart
It's a matter of life and death –
Protect health care
Switzerland, 2014
84 x 59.5 cm
MICR/BBT-2015-12-6

Unknown
Protecting human
dignity together
Lebanon, n.d.
33.5 x 49 cm
MICR/BBT-2010-58-2

Tom Stoddart →
It's a matter of life and deat
Violence against health car
must end
Switzerland, 2011
84 x 59.5 cm
MICR/BBT-2015-11-5

MY BABY DIDN'T DIE BECAUSE THE
MIDWIFE WAS KILLED IN AN EXPLOSION

MY BABY DIDN'T DIE BECAUSE
I WAS IN LABOUR FOR SUCH A LONG TIME

MY BABY DIED BECAUSE ARMED MEN HIJACKED
THE AMBULANCE COMING TO GET US

VIOLENCE AGAINST
HEALTH CARE MUST END

IT'S A
MATTER
OF LIFE
& DEATH

ICRC

Unknown
Child soldiers – The law says no!
Switzerland, 2002
84 x 59.5 cm
MICR/BBT-2015-13-6

Unknown
Families torn apart – The law says No!
Switzerland, 2002
84 x 59.5 cm
MICR/BBT-2015-13-8

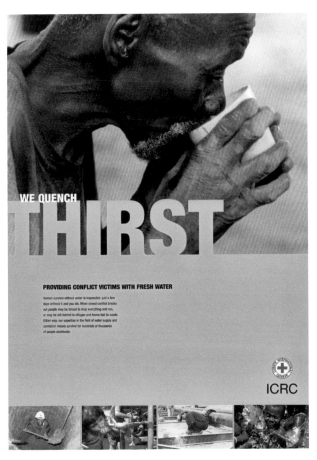

WE QUENCH
THIRST

PROVIDING CONFLICT VICTIMS WITH FRESH WATER

Human survival without water is impossible: just a few
days without it and you die. When armed conflict breaks
out people may be forced to drop everything and run,
or may be left behind in villages and towns laid to waste.
Either way, our expertise in the field of water supply and
sanitation means survival for hundreds of thousands
of people worldwide.

ICRC

Unknown
We quench thirst
Switzerland, 2001
84 x 59.5 cm
MICR/BBT-2001-89-2

Unknown
We bring hope
Switzerland, 2001
84 x 59.5 cm
MICR/BBT-2001-89-4

WE BRING
HOPE

ENSURING DETAINEES HAVE DECENT TREATMENT

Much of our work goes on behind closed doors: making
sure that people imprisoned for their involvement in armed
conflict are treated in an acceptable way. We work hard to
prevent or put an end to forced disappearances, torture
and other forms of ill-treatment, degrading conditions of
detention and loss of family contact. Helping to make
authorities act responsibly and treat security detainees
humanely brings a ray of light to those behind bars.
But for many the psychological release of seeing us at
regular intervals and knowing that we are concerned for
their welfare is the greatest relief we provide.

ICRC

Unknown
Only one thing stops
the Red Cross
New Zealand, 1999
63 x 84 cm
MICR/BBT-2000-120-4

THE IDEA FOR THE RED CROSS EMBLEM WAS BORN ON A BATTLEFIELD IN SOLFERINO IN 1859. TODAY IT STILL SEPARATES MEDICS FROM SOLDIERS, LIFE FROM DEATH. IT IS PROTECTED BY GENEVA CONVENTION AND TO MISUSE IT IS A CRIME UNDER LAW. IT DOESN'T BELONG ON A FIRST AID KIT. IT CAN'T BE USED BY VETS OR MEDICAL CENTRES. IT IS A SYMBOL OF PROTECTION, NEUTRALITY AND HUMANITY. THE NEW ZEALAND RED CROSS HAS A DUTY TO PROTECT IT, BECAUSE WITHOUT IT WE CAN'T PROTECT YOU.

Unknown
How to say "don't shoot me"
in 350 languages
New Zealand, 1999
63 x 84 cm
MICR/BBT-2000-120-3

163

Johan Sohlberg
*Stop! Don't touch! Do not touch
a mine or any other unknown
object! Mark the location and
inform the authorities!*
Azerbaijan, 1998
30 x 42 cm
MICR/BBT-2000-5-1-2

Unknown
Stop!
Anti-personnel mines
Colombia, n.d.
56 x 43.5 cm
MICR/BBT-1997-20-2

Unknown
Be careful – Mines are hidden!
Croatia, 1999
68 x 48 cm
MICR/BBT-2000-5-1-5

Unknown
*Stop! Be careful of anti-
personnel mines and explosive
devices. What should you
do? Stop, back away, mark
the spot, tell someone – mine
awareness campaign*
Mozambique, 1999
58 x 41 cm
MICR/BBT-2001-30-1

Unknown →
#NotATarget
Switzerland, 2017
128 x 90.5 cm
MICR/BBT-2017-34

Sliman Mansour
*Your body is a whole, keep it
in one piece. Stay away from
dangerous places and
suspicious objects*
Palestine, 2017
70 x 50 cm
MICR/BBT-2017-38-1

Kamal
*Danger – Be careful of war
machinery (mines, grenades,
non-explosive weapons)*
Yemen, 1995
72.5 x 50 cm
MICR/BBT-2000-189-7

Heinz-Jürgen Kristahn
*The Geneva Conventions –
The right to protection,
the duty to assist – Humanity
marked by neutrality –
For victims of war at sea*
Germany, 1981
84 x 59 cm
MICR/BBT-1986-28-41

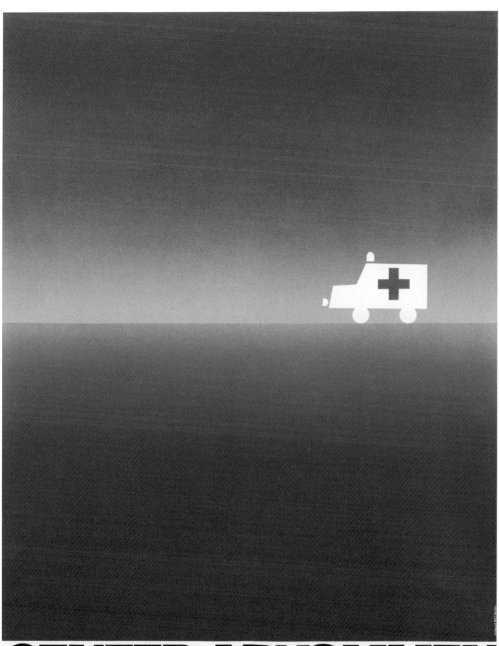

Heinz-Jürgen Kristahn
*The Geneva Conventions –
The right to protection,
the duty to assist –
Humanity marked by
neutrality – For victims
of war on land*
Germany, 1981
84 x 59 cm
MICR/BBT-1986-28-40

GENFER ABKOMMEN

RECHT AUF SCHUTZ – PFLICHT ZUR HILFE

MENSCHLICHKEIT IM ZEICHEN DER NEUTRALITÄT · FÜR KRIEGSOPFER ZU LAND

Unknown
Humanity protects nature –
Nature protects humanity
Republic of Korea, n.d.
53 x 37.5 cm
MICR/BBT-2003-22-42

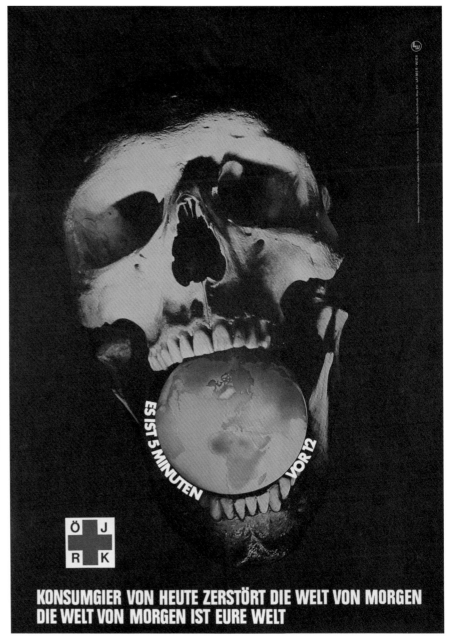

Unknown
The desire to consume today
destroys the world of tomorrow –
The world of tomorrow is
your world
Austria, n.d.
84 x 60 cm
MICR/BBT-2005-9-47

Unknown
*Our actions cause global
warming: let us join together –
contribute to reducing
greenhouse gases*
Madagascar, 2010
42 x 30 cm
MICR/BBT-2010-62-1

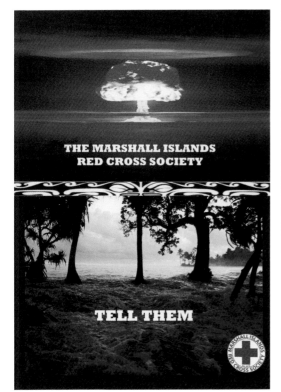

Unknown
Tell them
Marshall Islands, 2018
92 x 64 cm
MICR/BBT-2018-24-2

Unknown
*Your environment is your life...
protect it!*
Uganda, n.d.
42.5 x 59.5 cm
MICR/BBT-2002-24-91

Senior class B, Institution St. Paul
(school in St. Etienne, France)
*Road to peace – Limit your
aggression, no violence,
make room for discussion*
France, n.d.
30.5 x 44 cm
MICR/BBT-2002-29-87

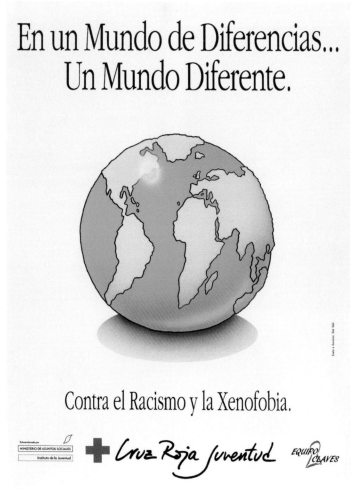

Diaz Rada
*In a world of
differences...
A different world – Against
racism and xenophobia –
Youth Red Cross*
Spain, 1992
70 x 50 cm
MICR/BBT-2010-20-16

Unknown
Understanding among peoples
Austria, n.d.
58.5 x 40.5 cm
MICR/BBT-2000-219-5

Biography

Roger Mayou

Roger Mayou studied at the Universities of Munich and Geneva, where he earned a Master's degree in Art History with a thesis on Body Art. He served as curator of the 19th- and 20th-century collections at the Musée d'Art et d'Histoire in Fribourg, Switzerland, producing exhibitions of Matisse's engravings, the Magnum photography cooperative, Alfred Hofkunst and "Splendours and Miseries of the Body", among others, all with accompanying catalogues.
He later worked as an art consultant for UBS in charge of the bank's collections, purchases and cultural sponsorship in French-speaking Switzerland.

He has been the director of the International Red Cross and Red Crescent Museum from 1998 until 2019, during which time he oversaw its expansion and transformation.
The Humanitarian Adventure, the museum's permanent exhibition since 2013, received the Kenneth Hudson Prize in 2015. He recently co-curated the exhibition *All too human: 20th and 21st century artists and suffering*.
He has chaired the Board of the University of Geneva and is currently a member of that university's strategic advisory board.

Catherine Burer

Catherine Burer holds Master's degrees in German and Art History from the University of Geneva. After teaching in secondary schools for several years, she worked as assistant curator at the International Red Cross and Red Crescent Museum when it was founded and opened, from 1986 to 1989. She then moved to Zurich, where she oversaw the poster collection at the Museum für Gestaltung Zürich from 1989 to 1997 and curated the exhibition *Kirei: Posters from Japan 1978–1993*. After moving back to Geneva, she worked for a private collector before returning, in 2009, to the International Red Cross and Red Crescent Museum, where she served as project coordinator during the museum's renovation. She has been the head of collections since 2015.

Valérie Gorin

Valérie Gorin earned a Master's degree in History in 2004 and a PhD in Communications and Media Studies in 2013, both from the University of Geneva. Her doctoral research was on photojournalism and humanitarian crises in American and French magazines from the 1960s to the 1990s.

She is currently a researcher and lecturer at the University of Geneva's Centre for Education and Research in Humanitarian Action (CERAH), Lausanne University and UniDistance off-site university.

Over the past several years, she has specialized in the history of humanitarian visual culture and NGOs' communication strategies, publishing numerous articles in French- and English-language publications such as the *Journal of Applied Journalism and Media Studies*, *European Review of History*, *Revue Suisse d'Histoire*, *Le Temps des Médias*, and *The International Review of the Red Cross*. She also contributed to an international exhibition on humanitarian icons during the World Humanitarian Summit in Istanbul in May 2016, with the Overseas Development Institute.

Martin Heller

Martin Heller was born in 1952 and lives between Zurich and Berlin. A cultural entrepreneur and curator, he is also the founder and chief executive of the Zurich-based company Heller Enterprises.

After studying at the Basel School of Decorative Arts and the University of Basel, he worked as museum curator and director at the Museum für Gestaltung (1986–1998) and the Museum Bellerive (1995–1998), both in Zurich. He then served as artistic director for the 2002 Swiss National Expo (1999–2003) and the city of Linz during its 2009 term as the European Capital of Culture (2005–2010). From 2011 to 2015, the Humboldt Forum in Berlin commissioned him to found and direct the Humboldt Lab Dahlem. Since 2003, he has worked as an author, exhibition curator, project manager, teacher and lecturer through Heller Enterprises. He is also a board member of Espazium, a publishing house specialized in architecture and culture.

musée + C genève
www.redcrossmuseum.ch

MIX
Paper from
responsible sources
FSC® C127663

International Red Cross and Red Crescent Museum

Editorial Director
Roger Mayou

Writers and poster selection
Catherine Burer, with Marie-Dominique De
Preter, Marie-Laure Berthier, Alessia Barbezat
and Sascha Bedoni

Poster search assistance
Grant Mitchell (FICR)

Graphic Design
Superposition / Vincent Schambacher
CHATSA / AlbanThomas

Photographs
Reprosolution / Olivier Pasqual

Translations
Christopher Scala and Rosie Wells (English),
Karin Siegenthaler (French), Anne Wölfli (French)

Other translations
Polat Abdullakhanov, Nodir Aminzoda,
Daiana Andreianu, Iharivelo Andriamambola,
Helen Baechler, Marie-Carmen Cubillos,
Aymeric De Preter, Thabsile Dlamini,
Marco Domingues, Johanna Gudmunds,
Rena Igarashi, Elzbetia Jkle, Leili Khaleghi,
Ludovic Kurer, Haide Laanemets, Orsolya Lakics,
HanGoo Lee, Nomin Orgodol, Bechir Mhancar,
M.J. Muradi, Pierre-Antoine Possa, Pavlina Trub,
Mary Vehkalahti, Peggy Wong

The museum is supported by
The Swiss Confederation,
the Federal Department of Foreign Affairs
The Republic and Canton of Geneva
The International Committee of the Red Cross
The International Federation of Red Cross and
Red Crescent Societies

Silvana Editoriale

Direction
Dario Cimorelli

Project Manager
Laurianne Barban

Art Director
Giacomo Merli

Editorial Coordinator
Sergio Di Stefano

Press Office
Lidia Masolini, press@silvanaeditoriale.it

ISBN: 9788836640843

International Red Cross
and Red Crescent Museum
Av. de la Paix 17
CH – 1202 Genève
www.redcrossmuseum.ch

Silvana Editoriale
Via dei Lavoratori, 78
IT – 20092 Cinisello Balsamo (Milano)
www.silvanaeditoriale.it

Reproductions, printing and binding in Italy
April 2019

Available through ARTBOOK | D.A.P.
155 Sixth Avenue, 2nd Floor, New York, N.Y. 10013
Tel: (212) 627-1999 Fax: (212) 627-9484

Schweizerische Eidgenossenschaft
Confédération suisse
Confederazione Svizzera
Confederaziun svizra

Département fédéral des
affaires étrangères DFAE

REPUBLIQUE
ET CANTON
DE GENEVE

POST TENEBRAS LUX

CICR

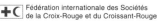
Fédération internationale des Sociétés
de la Croix-Rouge et du Croissant-Rouge